Living Hope:
"Lessons from the Book of 2 Timothy"

© By Dr. Randall D. Smith

These volumes were prepared with students and teachers of the Bible in mind. The series is taken from the actual teaching notes of Dr. Smith as he teaches through all of the Bible each year at Great Commission Bible Institute in Sebring, Florida.

Lessons in the Book of 2 Timothy
Living Hope

Lesson One: 2 Timothy 1:1-7 "A Fearless Look Ahead"

Key Principle: To mature to a grown follower of Jesus, I must learn to lay aside fear and shame, and pick up the banner of HOPE.

Lesson Two: 2 Timothy 1:8-18 "The Christian Optimist Manifesto"

Key Principle: To mature to a grown follower of Jesus, I must learn to see the future through the Word of God – the long view that restores hope when life is hard.

Lesson Three: 2 Timothy 2:1-26 "The Anchor"

Key Principle: To gain perspective and a godly attitude, fix your heart on some of the steadying examples that God has provided, and anchor your hope by following their pattern.

Lesson Four: 2 Timothy 3:1-17 "The Life Saver"

Key Principle: Our hope is not in historic moral victories or popular majorities but in timeless truths.

Lesson Five: 2 Timothy 4:1-5 "Four Keys to Unlock a Hopeful Outlook"

Key Principle: Our daily choices make the difference in living out hope.

Lesson Six: 2 Timothy 4:6-8 "Living in Certainty"

Key Principle: The hopeful mark of a believer is the statement of CERTAINTY about the future.

Lesson Seven: 2 Timothy 4:9-22 "Undistracted"

Key Principle: God's best work is accomplished in followers who learn to focus on the three eternal parts of life: people, the Word, and intimacy with God.

Table of Contents

Lessons in 2 Timothy
Living Hope:

Lesson One: 2 Timothy 1:1-7
"A Fearless Look Ahead"

If recent surveys are correct, many Americans are perhaps more afraid than they have ever been – at least since such things were measured and recorded. Fear seems a constant problem in our modern age. While we are less fearful of an airplane's safety, we have become more fearful of the TSA security procedures and what they may be doing with the "delicate" pictures they take of us. On the information front, some are more afraid of what the government is collecting about individuals while that government appears more afraid of what secrets a rogue government-cleared person may give to other nations. While some Americans are more afraid the authorities will move in to take away their guns, others are more afraid that someone with a gun will use one – particularly in sensitive areas like what happened in a California library a short time ago, or at Newtown, Connecticut last year. Some of those who carry smart phones are more afraid of the increased cost of their phone bill, while many others are more afraid of the bill amount they may face at their next dental appointment or doctor's visit. Yes, we seem to have made a life of great conveniences, and share that life with a constant companion named "fear."

Fear seems to be a modern fact of life. Yet, we have to admit something else even more uncomfortable than that fact. The truth is that fear isn't limited to people who DON'T KNOW AND WALK WITH GOD – everyone experiences it – though not necessarily to the same degree.

It's true that even those of us who have a long track record with the Master unwisely fall prey to our own emotions. Often I must remind myself that I can do ever so little about how I feel about something, but my actions must remain ever subject to my will. As a Christian, this is the reason for the urgency of constantly monitoring that will by God's expressed desire from His Word. When fallen natural desires are raised to the point of gaining control, the fundamental functions of self-control are thwarted. In that moment, I become a slave to my passions and a victim of my feelings. The regulating valve of my will is ignored, and I act out. God does not judge my feeling, for I have been born broken from the Fall, and even after my new life, I share a mind with the old man that must be put aside and starved of control. He does, however, judge the action, for that is a new sin – the act of handing control over to self that belongs to my King.

No matter how much has been invested in any of us, and no matter how much God has bestowed in gifts on our lives, even followers of Jesus can fail to produce the rightful fruit of such a blessed life because of **two simple problems: fear and shame**. The reason for both is the same… The bottom line is that God's moves don't always make sense to us. When we can't figure out what God is doing we are presented with a choice: shrink away from our faith or boldly recall all that God has done in the past and why He did it! The careful recollection of God's faithfulness and deliberate intention to trust in His care for the future are both wrapped up in the New Testament word translated "HOPE." As a believer, I am to live in HOPE and not in SHAME of the past or FEAR of the future.

Key Principle: To mature to a grown follower of Jesus, I must learn to lay aside fear and shame, and pick up the banner of HOPE.

That is part of my call to live like Jesus. He walked among men who feared, and the record of His ministry was one of COURAGE born of HOPE. It is important to note the biblical definition of "hope" is somewhat different from the modern usage – more akin to the use of it in terms of a young woman's HOPE CHEST. As she carefully places items in the box, she has every expectation they will one day serve her and her future husband. Hope in the *Bible* is "earnest expectation."

A young man named Timothy faced a time in his life when his life didn't come together. Things weren't going as well as he wanted them to. He had some good ideas, and some good intentions, but the church was facing larger and larger issues, and he was being drowned out in the process. He was struggling with his own nature and personality, and he was facing what looked to him to be defeat from a rising tide of persecution and trouble in the Roman world.

Paul, his mentor and teacher, had been arrested, faced the emperor, and was released. After some travels, Paul was picked up again – and this time Paul sounded like the end was near – his earth life was now on "borrowed time." Timothy saw his mentor fading, and knew the weight of ministry (in the human sphere) was about to fall to his generation of believers. Add to that, the emboldening of some who "acted out" during Paul's imprisonment in the Christian community, and Timothy was wearing out and losing hope.

God knew Tim's state, and so did Tim's mentor, the Apostle Paul. Both believed in Tim, but he needed both instruction and reassurance.

At the same time, it is clear that Timothy really did need to rethink some of his ministry and leadership practices. By reading carefully Paul's letters, we can grasp something of Timothy's symptoms and feel his problems:

- **He wasn't a fighter, and the fight was drawing closer.** He had to be prodded to fight the spiritual battle even though he wanted a back row seat (1 Tim. 1:18; 2 Tim. 1:6 "stir up the gift;" 2 Tim. 1:13 "grab what I taught you!").

- **He wasn't as focused as the times called for, and suffered from misdirected energy.** In particular, he had to be instructed to get the ladies settled down (He got them stirred up! 1 Tim. 2:11) He also engaged in discussions over his head (1 Tim. 6:20).

- **He suffered from a desire to be affirmed, perhaps due to a poor self-image.** He appears to have felt acute pressure because of his age and lack of experience (1 Tim. 4:11-12). He also seemed ready to ordain elders that weren't ready because of the pressure to be accepted by his (1 Tim. 5:19-22).

- **He didn't feel well**. His stomach was in knots (1 Tim. 5:23).

With physical and emotional challenges, the enemy was able to work on Timothy's spirit. Hope was slipping, little by little, and Timothy was becoming less effective. He needed someone or something to help him refocus. He was weakening, and there were signs of dropping productivity all around him. Maybe a believer who encounters this lesson today could use the same.

What can we do to regain focus, renew hope, and reject fear when things look down?

Look at the pattern from the first part of Paul's final letter to Timothy. Each word was carefully read and re-read by Timothy, every word precious to one whose hopes were fading.

Here is a pattern for regaining hope and chasing out fear:

First, open your heart to a godly friend and let them in. (2 Timothy 1:1-3)

For Tim, it was the letter from his mentor that opened his heart.

2 Timothy 1:1 Paul, an apostle of Christ Jesus by the will of God, according to the promise of life in Christ Jesus, 2 To Timothy, my beloved son: Grace, mercy and peace from God the Father and Christ Jesus our Lord. 3 I thank God, whom I serve with a clear conscience the way my forefathers did…

Notice the details of the opening, because they are important.

- *An apostle of Jesus Christ:* Paul was a tested messenger of God – his words had been tested and his lifestyle was known to be a fine example of godly character. Don't draw near to an untrusted or unreliable source of God's truth to regain hope and shake off fear.

- *…by the will of God:* Paul knew God's Word and was confident in God's plan. Don't expect a shaky believer to help you build back confidence. You need someone with the confidence to stand out. If you are hanging from a cliff, you want a strong arm to grab your wrists.

"Years ago, there was a test conducted by a university where 10 students were placed in a room. Three lines of varying length were drawn on a card. The students were told to raise their hands when the instructor pointed to the longest line. But 9 of the students had been instructed beforehand to raise their hands when the instructor pointed to the second longest line. One student was the stooge. The usual reaction of the stooge was to put his hand up, look around, and realizing he was all alone, pull it back down. This happened 75% of the time, with students from grade school through high school. The researchers concluded that many would rather stand with the majority than risk being right and alone. Now is the time when you will have to face some of your fears squarely with a firm confidence in God. Never, ever, take your cues from the crowd." (A-Z Sermon illustrations)

- *...according to the promise of life:* Look for someone who focuses you on God's promises, not more of Earth's problems. Don't find someone who will add to your woes their own set of complaints. I am thankful to the Lord that I have a few friends who know well how to get from God the strength to move through troubled times. We all need the longer view when life starts pulling us down.

Just this week I experienced this. I remembered thinking it strange that though I am on the Earth for but a few moments, I seem to so quickly wrap myself in the pain of its every turn. I read an obituary of a good man that I admired and was reminded again: "Stop your worrying, Randy. This is your Father's world. It is not yours to fix, nor is it yours to pollute. He was spinning planets long before you awoke the first time, and He will accomplish His story to the last detail." Yes, it was again time for me to remember, relax, and let God run things. That is one of the things I love about living in my Father's shadow. I can rest knowing He has everything covered.

Note how confident Paul was about God's work and his future. Just a few verses later he wrote:

2 Timothy 1:12 For this reason I also suffer these things, but I am not ashamed; for I know whom I have believed and I am convinced that He is able to guard what I have entrusted to Him until that day.

The Apostle Paul used the Greek term *paratheke* for the term "entrusted." The term meant "a treasure or a deposit left with someone you trust completely." Since banking was only available in the client–patronage system, wealth was often deposited with friends or family based on trust. As a result, the person you asked to take care of your possessions was someone you knew well, and trusted completely.

Conquering fear is not simply a matter of self-determination; it is a matter of dependence on the amount of love and trust we truly place in our God.

Several years ago, an experiment on endurance was conducted at the University of California at Berkeley. The experiment involved placing Norwegian field rats in a tub of water, where they were forced to swim until they grew exhausted and finally drowned. During the first experiment, the researchers discovered that on the average, these rats were capable of swimming for over seven hours before drowning. A second experiment was conducted, exactly like the first but with one exception. This time, when a rat was getting too exhausted to swim any longer, the researchers would remove the rat from the tub of water for a few seconds, then put the rat back into the water to continue swimming. These rats were able to swim for almost 20 hours before perishing. The researchers concluded that the rats in the second group were able to swim so much longer than the first group because of one factor: they had HOPE. They had experienced a rescue—and what kept them going was the HOPE that they would be rescued again. (Edited from, *More Hot Illustrations for Youth Talks,* by Wayne Rice. Copyright 1995, *Youth Specialties, Inc.)*

- *To Timothy, my beloved son:* Draw into your confidence someone that has your best interest at heart – one that knows and loves you. Solitary Christians wither because we are called to be part of a body. At the same time, it is wise to choose carefully those who become a part of your deeper life and those who hear your inner discouragements. They need to be strong, but they need to truly LOVE you. In discouragement, you don't need to invite Job's friends. Any normal person would have ended their life surrounded by men like that!

You can hear Paul's love, even as the letter progresses. Skip down a few verses and we read: *2 Tim. 1:4 ...longing to see you, even as I recall your tears, so that I may be filled with joy.*

- *Grace, mercy and peace from God:* Make sure your friend will draw his strength from God's empowering and his answers from God's Word. There will never be a more important time to have a friend who is deeply entrenched in studying and knowing God's Word than when you are in a crisis of hope.

Years ago I recall hearing a pastor offer this thought: On day six of the ill-fated mission of Apollo 13, the astronauts needed to make a critical course correction. If they failed, they might never return to Earth. To conserve power, they shut down the onboard computer that steered the craft. Yet the astronauts needed to conduct a thirty-nine-second burn of the main engines. How to steer? Astronaut Jim Lovell determined that if they could keep a fixed point in space in view through their tiny window, they could steer the craft manually. That focal point turned out to be their destination—Earth. Apollo 13, for thirty-nine agonizing seconds, was directed by Lovell focused on keeping Earth in view. By not losing sight of that reference point, the three astronauts avoided disaster.

Scripture reminds us that to finish your life mission successfully, *Fix your eyes on Jesus, the author and perfecter of our faith"* (Heb. 12:2). That is how Paul was re-energized. He didn't look at the news, and he didn't look at the church – he looked at the Master.

- *...Whom I serve with a clear conscience*: Pick someone who has a clear account with God. You don't need someone counseling you who is doing penance or passing through some purifying transformation due to guilt. He may have a past (Paul surely did), but he needs to be clear-headed and free of a guilty conscience to direct you back to God and restore hope.

Yes, draw in a friend – but not just any friend.

- He should be a tested messenger of God with a track record of knowledge and confidence in God's Word.
- He should be someone who deeply cares about you, and knows how to refresh and renew himself in God's hands.
- He should have a clean heart and a clear conscience.

If that friend isn't these things, he won't fit the pattern of the friend you are looking for. He may make you laugh, and you may enjoy time with him– but he won't really be what you need. If you don't have one – ask God to help you to begin to build that kind of bond with a person who knows and loves Him.

Second, find some strong prayer support. (2 Timothy 1:3b)

2 Timothy 1:3b ...as I constantly remember you in my prayers night and day.

In Timothy's case, one of his prayer-warriors was the same friend that we have been describing, but that isn't essential. There is no biblical demand that the same person who is praying is the one who God is using to answer your need for counsel and direction. God calls all of us to pray for one another – but has NOT called all of us to counsel one another.

Prayer verbally reminds us that God is in control – so we must not only accept prayer – but we must PRAY as well. Reminded of God's control, we can face our fears. He gives us the ability to do what life demands, to love when others hate, and to be under control when others throw restraint to the winds.

Third, look back at God's blessings in your past. (2 Timothy 1:5-6)

2 Timothy 1:5 For I am mindful of the sincere faith within you, which first dwelt in your grandmother Lois and your mother Eunice, and I am sure that it is in you as well. 6 For this reason, I remind you to kindle afresh the gift of God which is in you through the laying on of my hands.

Don't look past the good hand of God in how you got where you are. God has been at work, even before you knew it. You were formed by His hand, and sculpted for a unique purpose. Looking back can help us remember that dark nights have new dawns that follow.

Paul reminded Tim of two past features of God's work:

First, there was the godly heritage that Timothy had, a faith demonstrated in his grandmother and then in his mother. What a blessing for those who have it as I did. Yet, even if you did not grow up in good circumstances – there is a pathway of blessing if you look back in your life.

Second, Paul drew Tim into a mental picture of a moment – some years before – where Paul and other leaders laid hands on Timothy and acknowledged that God had both gifted and empowered him to do the very task with which he was now struggling. You may not have been called to pastor a group of people, and you may never have had such a "laying on of hands" as this. At the same time, you may look back and recall a time when those you love claimed out loud the nature of your giftedness, or entrusted you with serious and important tasks, showing their confidence.

Fourth, inventory the ingredients "driving" your life choices. (2 Timothy 1:7)

2 Timothy 1: 7 For God has not given us a spirit of timidity, but of power and love and discipline.

There are some ingredients of life that God did not put there. There are others that He intends for us to have as a part of our experience. Paul offered to Tim an inventory of these.

- Paul made it clear that God did not add to our lives FEAR (*delia* or *di-lee'-ah* is actually the word for timidity or paralyzing reticence). He desires REVERENCE, as in the fear of the Lord that is the beginning of knowledge – but that is not this kind of reticence, but rather a firm grasp of respect for His position as Creator and Ruler.
- Paul makes clear that three specific ingredients have been added to Timothy's life to make him productive in his life and ministry. These three ingredients are
-

  ❖ **Power: the term is *dunamis*, from which we get the name "dynamite."**

It literally means our "**ability to perform as required.**" In the life of the believer, God adds the power to achieve what is needed for our sanctification and preparation for Heaven (glorification). The term is used 120 times in the NT, and is a well-known ingredient in the believer's life. In other words, believers may lack the will to obey God and grow in Him, but they do not lack the empowering to become what He desires of them. If we are honest, most of the time in our lives that we say we "cannot" we actually mean we "will not" because we do not sufficiently desire to do so.

Let's be absolutely clear: you and I who know Jesus as Savior have the God-given power to resist sin and the enemy – and walk with God.

  ❖ **Love: the term is agape is a familiar one to followers of Jesus.**

Agapáō in antiquity meant, "to prefer." Our practical definition of the word is born of its functional uses in Scripture. It is "acting deliberately to meet a need, because there is a need, expecting nothing in return. In that sense, it is to "prefer" another before self. It is the soul of "other-person-centeredness." It was the word for God's motivation to send His Son to die in our place. In other words, God not only empowered us in sanctification, He also added back into the fallen selfish being, an impulse to act on behalf of others as Jesus did for us. It must be fostered and grown – but the ability to do it is part of God's additions to our life in Christ. You and I have the impulse, if allowed to rise to the surface, to care for others with a love that is otherwise impossible to explain in human terms.

> ❖ **Sound Mind: the term is *so-fron-is-mos'* – derived from the word for properly moderate, issuing in prudent and sensible behaviors that "fit" a situation.**

It is the "sound reasoning" of one dominated by God's agenda and Spirit. Believers were given the ability to reason from God's Word and apply its words to life. There are ways this ingredient can be thwarted from producing its desired effects – as with power and love. It can be dulled by inebriation, constant anesthetizing, or the dulling effects of certain stimuli – as in some games. Yet, if nurtured and encouraged, it can be sharpened. You and I have the ability to navigate life with God's Word as a map, and God's Spirit as a guide.

Therefore, with paralyzing reticence discarded, believers are empowered to put away bondage to sin, to heighten our sensitivity to others and their needs, and to keenly apply God's truth to our daily lives.

That is true because God has done what is necessary to add into our lives the empowering, sensitivity, and revealed truth.

Pastor David Ward wrote in a message called *Gospel without Walls* these words: "Russell Moore recounts a conversation with the evangelical theologian Carl Henry. As Moore and some of his friends were lamenting the miserable shape of the church, they asked Dr. Henry if he saw any hope in the coming generation of evangelicals. Dr. Henry replied, "Of course, there is hope for the next generation of evangelicals. But the leaders of the next generation might not be coming from the current evangelical establishment. They are probably still pagans. Who knew that Saul of Tarsus was to be the great apostle to the Gentiles? Who knew that God would raise up a C. S. Lewis or a Charles Colson? They were unbelievers who, once saved by the grace of God, were mighty warriors for the faith." Russell Moore added, "The next Jonathan Edwards might be the man driving in front of you with the Darwin Fish bumper decal. The next Charles Wesley might be a misogynist, profane hip-hop artist right now. The next Billy Graham might be passed out drunk in a fraternity house right now. The next Charles Spurgeon might be making posters for a Gay Pride March right now. The next Mother Teresa might be managing an abortion clinic right now." (Sermon central illustrations)

You see,

- Hope is restored when **I remember the power of God to change people**.
- Hope is renewed when I remember **this life isn't the center of everything** – HEAVEN IS.

I love this story:

"A football game was being played in Badger Stadium in 1982 in Madison, Wisconsin with more than 60,000 fans in attendance. The home team was losing. Out of the blue, during time outs, when play was at a stop, the fans would jump up and roar with excitement. Why? Many of those in the stadiums were listening to a game being broadcast on the radio from 70 miles down the road. What they were listening to was the Milwaukee Brewers beating the St. Louis Cardinals in game three of the 1982 World Series. Their team on the field was losing, but they were tuned into something better down the road. The Christian life is like that for us today. Our circumstances are bad at times but we must be tuned into something better down the road. We must place our hopes not in this world but in Heaven." (From a sermon by Tommy Burrus, *Dealing with Discouragement,* 7/1/2009, sermon central)

To mature to a grown follower of Jesus, I must learn to lay aside fear and shame, and pick up the banner of HOPE.

Lessons in 2 Timothy
Living Hope:

Lesson Two: 2 Timothy 1:8-18
"The Christian Optimist Manifesto"

To truly embrace Christ, to truly have become a Christian, to believe all that the truth of Jesus' coming, His death, and His promises of the future – is to become an unstoppable optimist.

There are many voices of people who have claimed Christ as Savior that sound very pessimistic. I challenge you to see through a flawed logic. If Jesus is King, and if He died for me – if He rose from the dead and broke the power of death, and if He is, in fact, right now preparing a place for me as He promised – life is only getting better. As each moment ticks by on the clock above, my full redemption draws nearer. The Earth around me grows closer to a judgment followed by a purging that will yield a new and wondrous place. The assailing of my flesh by corruption and illness is nearing its end. The railing of rebellion is reaching toward its final breath. My Savior is fashioning my next home, my next experience in joyful delight.

As Ted Dekker wrote in *The Slumber of Christianity: Awakening a Passion for Heaven on Earth*, "The world's bumper sticker reads: Life sucks, and then you die. Perhaps Christian bumper stickers should read: Life sucks, but then you find hope and you can't wait to die."

Deeply rooted in the physical life around us and its happiness, many Christians appear to have "left the reservation" to the land of the pessimists. The subtle adoption of a pagan worldview has caused them to measure life by the short stick – the here and now. Yet, on closer inspection to the Word of God, Jesus called us to measure life by the longer view – His eventual triumph over all things. The New Testament doesn't close with the instructional epistles that show the flaws of men – even those who love Jesus. It doesn't close with warnings of the doom of the Earth, a zombie apocalypse in waiting, but rather it closes with a warning not to carve off a single word of the true end of all things from the story – Jesus shall reign. The Creator shall stand vindicated for His plan, and finally understood and acknowledged by all His creation. The scene ends with knees bowed and confessing tongues.

Key Principle: To mature to a grown follower of Jesus, I must learn to see the future through the Word of God – the long view that restores hope when life is hard.

I am not saying things are looking rosy in the short term. The so-called "Age of Enlightenment" (also called the "Age of Reason") promised the world the opposite of the *Bible* – a world solved of its ills by the enthroned human will standing above the dullard mythologists who believed in a "god." This cultural movement of intellectuals in the 17th and 18th centuries rose with the purpose to reform society using reason, but at the same time pushing society from a framework of ideas grounded in tradition and faith. It sought to advance knowledge solely through the scientific method – because the human brain replaced the revelation of any divine source. It was deeply embedded in the worldview as a struggle for human development in opposition to faith. This is not a history lesson. This godless ideology is on the march with renewed vigor through our universities again, and has found voice in our modern American courts and media outlets. Think carefully about the words of this author:

"How beautiful it all seemed at the time of the Enlightenment, that man triumphant would bring to pass that earthly paradise whose groves of academe would ensure the realization forever of peace, plenty, and beatitude in practice. But what a nightmare of wars, famines, and folly was to result therefrom." (Malcolm Muggeridge, *The End of Christendom*)

It has produced a world that believes saving whales is intrinsically more moral and more essential than saving unborn humans, and delivering people from hearing a message about the sting of judgment more vital than doing what is moral as defined by their Creator. It was deeply rooted into the plan of the "Great Society" that is now yielding its fruits – an amoral individualist with little rationale for standing on any absolute "truth." They called for greater assistance for the needy and got generations of people who have believe public assistance is both a guaranteed right and equal in all respect to their "job." They constructed a worldview that redefines inconvenient as wrong and statement of truth as intolerant judgment. All this they offered with great hopeful optimism in the alternative view of man's origin, purpose and destiny.

Yet the Christian view of life is not primarily fixed in the here and now. Ours is a message that man CANNOT fix himself – for what is broken is within, just as our Savior clearly said. Ours is a message that BROKEN MEN need not reform themselves by some religious work or radical self-deprivation. Ours is message that Jesus saves. He died in our place, and offers us new life when we give our lives to Him. His life then flows within us – and His message of truth carefully begins its transforming work in us. It is not our work – it is His. At the same time, the destination of my life was dramatically altered by the grasp of Jesus on my heart. I have Heaven in the future and transformation in the present. I am a child of God, and I am learning to act like it, while I anticipate a soon coming journey to my Father's house! What a life is mine!

Now, I admit that even some believers will object and claim there are pessimists and there are optimists in life – it is a personality thing. I do not agree. I believe that salvation brings new life, and new life brings a new narrative of my end. I am not optimistic because men are getting better. I am optimistic because I believe the end story of the *Bible* – the Creator shall stand unopposed and victorious – and I have committed my days and my future in this life and beyond to Him. I believe, therefore, the message of William Ralph Inge when he said, "No Christian can be a pessimist, for Christianity is a system of radical optimism."

Christian optimism doesn't believe men will get better, but rather that their rebellion will continue, and in fact grow in strength and audacity. It accepts the biblical idea that such a growing darkness will come with that overt rebellion that God will clearly make His point: Man cannot fix himself.

Let me say it unmistakably: **I truly believe that rationalism, humanism and enlightenment will eventually be exposed for more deceptions of the same voice – Lucifer's song of mutiny and self-love.** Science will scoff at the notion that they are beset by the same flaws of any philosophy – but they will prove unable to reform the broken nature of man. They will prove unable to bring real HOPE when terrible tragedies strike, for their power ends at the last breath of physical life. There is nothing beyond but in the memories of those who remain. Bonhoeffer was right: If you board the wrong train, it is no use running along the corridor in the other direction. Our world is destined to move in a direction so anti-god, that hope in this Earth will drain.

Yet, we are optimists. We smile and look up, for redemption draws near. Not only that, but I stand in a world accompanied by the Author of hope. Look back at 2 Timothy 1 and listen to the words of an apostle calling from a prison cell, facing a sword to the neck. He is none other than the Apostle Paul, and his message is bathed in sweat, stench, and a sad state of companions. At the same time, it is a message of TRUE HOPE.

In the last study, we learned that Paul recalled for Tim a series of **things that should have helped restore hope:**

- **First, Tim had in Paul a godly friend that believed in him.** (2 Tim 1:1-3a)

If ever there was a good example of a godly friend that could point upward, Paul was that guy in Tim's life. If you have such a friend, breathe a prayer of thanks for them right now!

- **Second, Tim had strong prayer support.** (2 Tim. 1:3b)

The battles we fight are not merely in the flesh – but spiritual ones that show up in the physical world. They cannot be addressed by mere force of will to follow a list of resolutions – that doesn't account for the spiritual world. Prayer is the effective tool to remind us that we are not alone, and that our God is able to supply when things look too difficult to see that.

- **Third, Tim could look back at God's blessings in his past.** (2 Tim. 1:5-6) **He had a great family heritage.**

Paul called on Tim to recall that God was at work in him before Tim was even aware of it – and that is true of all of us!

- **Fourth, Tim should inventory the ingredients driving life choices** (2 Tim. 1:7) **– he was to remove fear and recognize the deliberate ingredients God put in him as power, love and a sound mind.**

It is easy to be driven by FEAR, but it is not GODLY BEHAVIOR. Our Master gave us the power to stand against sin, the sensitivity to reckon the hurting around us, and the sound reasoning to grab the truths of His Word and live them out.

How could Paul, who was facing the end of his life, exude hope and offer encouragement? Because he measured life by the longer stick found in the Word of God.

Paul knew Jesus wasn't done when the Empire ruled against his life. He knew that His Savior wasn't losing His grip on the world when his body was tossed into a dungeon… and he urged Tim to see life that way as well. He told Timothy – as his mentor and his friend – to do seven things to move ahead in HOPE:

Practical Commands to Show Restored Hope:Stop fearing opposition. (2 Tim. 1:8-9)

2 Timothy 1:8 Therefore do not be ashamed of the testimony of our Lord or of me His prisoner, but join with me in suffering for the gospel according to the power of God, 9 Who has saved us and called us with a holy calling, not according to our works, but according to His own purpose and grace which was granted us in Christ Jesus from all eternity.

Because God didn't give Tim the fear that he had – he needed to boot it out of his life! He needed to deliberately and consciously coach his own heart to recognize his God-given power to deny his flesh, while growing in sensitivity to hurting people and acute awareness of the principles of God's Word. On that basis, as recorded in 1:7, Tim was to put aside any sense of SHAME that he felt because his mentor shared a cell with murderers and wretched men. He was to shed any DISGRACE over following a crucified Criminal – for that was merely the arrogant evaluation of the Creator by the broken creation.

Paul called Tim back to the foundational truth – Jesus saved him by suffering on his behalf. He was NOT supposed to shrink away from the public connection to Jesus and to Paul. He was, rather, supposed to recall that his salvation came with a HOLY CALLING – a mark of separation from the world. That calling wasn't given to him based on his accomplishments, nor was it based on any life goal that Tim may have felt before Jesus changed his life. Tim was to stop fearing the opposition Jesus faced before, and Paul was facing at the time of the writing. He was to see that he had a call from Jesus that was to dominate his actions and reactions – no matter what course the world took.

Grab the eternal perspective to see real life! (2 Tim. 1:10-11)

2 Timothy 1:10 ...but now has been revealed by the appearing of our Savior Christ Jesus, Who abolished death and brought life and immortality to light through the gospel, 11 for which I was appointed a preacher and an apostle and a teacher.

Paul faced the loss of his head, but he did not face death. His body they would kill – but he was more than a body. <u>That is at the heart of the Christian message. We are not just physical beings – we are primarily spiritual beings with a short stint of physical life.</u> At the end of all the educational and intellectual posturing of our day – man without a Savior still has no real solution for the six foot hole he is facing at the end – but Jesus does. He has been there and back, and He holds the keys to death and true life.

The apostle recognized that he was appointed to teach that very truth – Jesus conquered death. When John wrote from Patmos that he had seen the risen Christ, he reported Jesus' words:

Revelation 1:17b ...Do not be afraid. I am the First and the Last. 18 I am the Living One; I was dead, and now look, I am alive for ever and ever! And I hold the keys of death and Hades.

"Do not be afraid," Jesus said. "I control life and death, and I control the end of the story!" That is either the truth or a bold-faced lie. If it is true – we need not fear if we KNOW JESUS.

Check the internet and it is flooded with skeptics and cynics over this claim of the New Testament. They are sure they have so advanced in technical civilization, having gone "all the way to the moon" to land their feet and "touch the face of God" they can now pull down the Creator to answer to them, and force Him to show Himself in terms they can accept. In arrogance, they fail to look out into space and see how little of it they have actually traversed.

They sit in certainty that such things as recorded in the *Bible* cannot happen for such a Creator does not exist. Yet the heavens declare exquisite design. The human body screams that it is a product of intricate enterprise. "Millions of years!" they shout. "With millions of years, we can see the great emergence of evolving design!" For that belief, in lab coats they ask men to place faith in their conclusions, while mocking the very notion of the metaphysical as primitive mythology. This begs the question... "Why? Why should there be design with no intentional designer working behind it? Why should there be growth and expansion of good characteristics? *Cui bono*? (To what end or purpose?)

If that isn't enough, there is even a greater question: "Why should I care? If there is no purpose, no forethought, no destiny, nothing beyond my decades walking on the planet – where is the hope at the grave of a child? How can I lift the soul of a friend who has lost the love of their life? Robbed of purpose and destiny, how can I not sink into despair at the sight of the cemetery as I drive by?

If the design that I see in the world about me has not an intentional hand, and man stands in the light of no judge but himself, his peers, and posterity – how compelling is the case for me to deny earthly pleasures and learn self-control for some temporary version of the 'common good'? If no personal God exists, and no judgment follows this life, if it is true that the fittest survive and that is the way of the ages, let us cease this nonsense of good behavior and simply seek to become the strongest of all in order that we may reap the benefits of that strength in the short life we have on the planet. Why deny the urge to take food from the weak that I may be full? Would reputation or memory stop me? Achilles knew that fame has no meaning beyond this life – and the memorial of posterity is an empty promise. The fact is, most Americans don't know one quarter of the names of the men who led their country, though it is not all that old a place. Memories are short, and it isn't worth denying myself to be remembered as a good man.

There is something else I know about people: **Without a judge man will not behave any better than he drives when he thinks no one is watching the highway.** Without a purpose to human history, man will slowly move downward to feed his baser instincts and sensual pleasures. Things won't get better. With every freedom and right, someone else will suffer. Divorce will become easy, but children will suffer from increased lack of parental tender bonding. Marriage will be redefined, but family will be a word so overused and under-defined it will cease to have certain meaning. Children will be allowed to be born when it is convenient, and elderly will be ended when their life no longer makes economic sense. This is the bright new world of the enlightened heart.

Let me say it with unmistakable clarity: Jesus rendered death inoperable to those who know Him. That is the term ABOLISH in 2 Timothy 1:10. The *Bible* openly proclaims there is a PURPOSE, there is a DESIGNER, I have a DESTINY. Bill and Gloria Gaither said it well, "Because He lives, I can face tomorrow. Because He lives, all fear is gone. Because I know He holds the future, life is worth the living, just because He lives!"

Trust that Jesus knows how to handle your future since He made you! (2 Tim. 1:12)

2 Timothy 1:12 For this reason I also suffer these things, but I am not ashamed; for I know whom I have believed and I am convinced that He is able to guard what I have entrusted to Him until that day.

I mentioned last time the Greek word, *paratheke* that is the "treasure or deposit left with someone you trust completely."

Here was Paul's point to Tim: "Trust Jesus with all you have. He won't let you down, Tim... I have. I know He will care for me, and it is my neck about to go on the chopping block."

Conquering fear is not just about quelling an emotion – it is about exchanging it with the confidence that comes from depending of God in the most practical ways. Maybe someone here wants to ask what I am certain Tim wanted to ask so long ago..."How do you do replace FEAR with TRUST like that?" Keep reading the text, Paul wasn't done...

What is clear in verse 12 is that it starts with understanding what the Scripture teaches about the Person of God. You do it by recognizing that God does not place you in pain without purpose. That isn't His nature. Trouble doesn't come because God is cruel toward His children... That isn't it.

Dr. David Osborn at Denver Seminary said a few years ago, "Too often, we try to use God to change our circumstances, while He is using our circumstances to change us. You see, God is right now in the process of making us like Christ. Think of the process of refining maple syrup. Maple trees are tapped with buckets hung under the taps, and out drips a sap, which is thin and clear, like water. On a good day, 50 trees will yield 30-40 gallons of sap, but it is essentially useless at this point with only a hint of sweetness. Then as the buckets fill, they are emptied into large bins that sit over an open fire. The sap comes to a slow boil; and as it boils, its water content is reduced and its sugars are concentrated. Hours later, it has developed a rich flavor and golden-brown color, but it must be strained several times to remove impurities before being reheated, bottled, and graded for quality. In the end, those 30-40 gallons of sap are reduced to one gallon of pure, delicious maple syrup, which is far better than the cheap, imitation, colored sugar-water that passes for maple syrup in the grocery store. So it is when we come to faith in Christ. We start like raw, unfinished sap, which could have been tossed aside as worthless. But God knew what He could make of us. He sought and found us, and His skillful hands are transforming us into something precious, sweet and useful. The long and often painful refining process brings forth a pure, genuine disciple easily distinguished from cheap imitations." (Michele Straubel, Red Lake, Minnesota, from a sermon by C. Philip Green, *Our Living Hope*, 4/26/2011)

Recognize the treasure of the Word of God. (2 Tim. 1:13)

2 Timothy 1:13 Retain the standard of sound words which you have heard from me, in the faith and love which are in Christ Jesus.

If trust begins with understanding what God's Word says about God's Person, the issue of the Word's truthfulness comes to the fore. Timothy was to see the words taught him by Paul as the precious treasure of God's Holy Truth, and he was to highly prize each one. He was to learn the Word, trust the Word, and keep the Word ever close. As the world's darkness pressed in, Tim would need a lamp for his feet and light for his path.

How long will it take us to learn that time away from God's Word is time away from understanding life from God's perspective? How we perceive the world is a product of what we see – and God's Word is a lamp to the heart to show the dangerous obstacles to walking well, as well as a beacon to help others be drawn to God through our testimony. We must learn that the *Bible* is precious, as essential a part of our daily regimen as our toothbrush and our deodorant. If you can go away for a week and don't think you'll need a *Bible* with you – it is likely that others can tell in your life. Just because you passed the "sniff test" on your own – doesn't mean your life isn't truly offensive.

We must guard by the Spirit's power the timeless truths placed in our hands. (2 Tim. 1.14)

2 Timothy 1:14 Guard, through the Holy Spirit who dwells in us, the treasure which has been entrusted to you.

The idea here is that <u>each generation of believers will need to protect the legacy of the text, and rightly reflect the principles of God's truth.</u> Compromise may bring short-term popularity and likeability – but long term devastation. There is no time like now that this has been more important. Any forum discussing God's view of marriage and sexuality is now filled with people who claim to be believers but utterly misquote and improperly frame key principles of God's Word on the vital issues facing the American home. We must be sharp on truth and loving in delivery. The church is sending mixed messages, because the Scriptures have not been carefully learned, studied and applied.

How do we reflect TRUTH but still show LOVE? That is a good question.

First, <u>we need to understand that LOVE is not the wholesale nod of approval to anyone who wants to feel included and accepted.</u> My love for my wife has an unspoken and never violated rule that she remain separate for me alone. I am not open to redefining that term for the sake of love.

Second, <u>we must remember the ultimate objective of our teaching is not to tell people what we think about all the issues of our day, but to help connect them with biblical truth on the way to connecting to God Himself.</u> We would do well to separate ideas into three important categories:

- Absolutes (unchanging principles of God's Word)
- Convictions (culturally sensitive applications of principle that are not universally agreed upon even by brothers and sisters in the faith)
- Preferences (traditional methods that we like)

If we spend our energies on the last two, we will not address the first one – and that is where the power for God's Word can move effectively into the hardened heart – just as it did for all of us who believe.

We must recognize many of us have been duped into distraction inside our own respective worship communities. Some are caught up in peripheral struggles of stylistic issues in the church while the mammoth battle of changing worldviews is not being addressed – let alone strategically fought. Scores of churches are losing their children, but they fail to see why, claiming an issue like drums or hymnbooks – when this is far from the real problem.

Make note: When a church ignores the grave issues of worldview but rages about lesser issues of style, preference, and tradition it is setting itself up to grey first, close later. **Spiritual bloodletting on preference leaves little energy to fight the real battles of our day.**

Third, we must awaken to the reality that we live in a culture largely committed to relativism, unreceptive toward all-embracing, unchanging, and ultimate truth. That makes the *Bible* as understood and presented by Christians in the public square an offense of its own, regardless of the content and irrespective of our quality of presentation. Some of this offensiveness simply can't be avoided without compromising the spirit of the text. We need to simply accept that fact, and at the same time not grow angry or withdraw from our society because of the hardness toward truth. As God said long ago to the Prophet Samuel, they aren't rejecting the messenger, but the Master and His mastery. They are responding to a much choreographed entertainment industry and a carefully sculpted educational system designed by pagan and post-modern minds.

Nil desperandum – don't despair. It is still very possible to gain a hearing for the gospel in a relativistic setting, and our cause is not dead and neither is our God now helpless. The Author is still the Finisher. There are things we can and must do and the Gospel will find its mark in some. We must guard truth for the sake of coming generations – even if they have little place for it in their lives right now. Nothing is made better or stronger by whining – but the fervent and effectual prayer of one who walks with God pierces the armor of the enemy with the power and principles of God.

We must face the struggles and troubles that come from working among weak men. (1:15)

2 Timothy 1:15 You are aware of the fact that all who are in Asia turned away from me, among whom are Phygelus and Hermogenes.

Discouragement will feed fear, and fear will block faith. How we handle trouble is a key point for the world to see our testimony. We must expect men to defect. We must anticipate that some will invite embrace sin and call it love. Others will strike parts from their *Bible* they perceive are not palatable to the post-modern mind. They will speak of blessing, love, and tolerance – but know little of surrender, repentance, and mourning over sin.

When it happens, remember this: It isn't new – this has always been around. Misuse of the Word accompanied proper instruction from the first century. As God poured out healing power through an apostle, a huckster tried to buy the power for self-benefit. As God communicated through His Spirit, others tried to mimic the conditions. We can trace their path all the way back to Moses and Aaron throwing down a rod and picking up a snake. The problem of fakery isn't new, and it isn't slyer than before – if you know the Lord, walk by His Spirit, and study carefully His Word.

Don't judge too harshly those who feel forced to point out the names of ministries and teachers that aren't walking in truth. It sounds "judgy" but Paul found it necessary to make his point to Tim – and we may, on occasion, need to do it as well. We reserve it for the most egregious cases of violation - but we do it when it is needful.

Finally, we must "bathe often" in praise for the blessings God has put in our life. (1:16)

2 Timothy 1:16: The Lord grant mercy to the house of Onesiphorus, for he often refreshed me and was not ashamed of my chains; 17 but when he was in Rome, he eagerly searched for me and found me— 18 the Lord grant to him to find mercy from the Lord on that day— and you know very well what services he rendered at Ephesus.

Paul's hope was in the deliverance that JESUS would give him in his death, but his endurance in the physical torment was boosted by the little reprieves he got from Onesiphorus.

The man whose name means, "profit bringer" is mentioned only two times in the New Testament (see also 2 Timothy 4:19). God used this man to become a friend of Paul when desperately in need of one. Onesiphorus took a profound risk seeking out the imprisoned apostle who brought the Word to the people Asia – his hometown crowd. Paul met him and believed God had sent him a very special relief in the midst of the hard time he faced. How he celebrated godly and bold friends in the midst of his deprivations! God hadn't forgotten to send a small cup of water to his parched and pained soul.

What did Paul do?

- He praised.
- He thanked God.
- He acknowledged the diligence of the man who sought him out.
- He kept his focus, not on the encroachment of evil, but on the actions of Godly helpers.

Let me deliberately ask you to do something before we close this lesson: Make sure that as much of your effort is found in praising God and trumpeting good as preaching warning and pinpointing evil. The world will notice a positive voice – they truly will.

Beloved, we are a people made for the hope that is found in Jesus Christ.

God created us, bought us, indwelt us, instructed us, and is transforming us… but we are making a mistake when we move to playing defense instead of working from a victorious HOPE.

In his book, *Winning Life's Toughest Battles*, psychologist Julius Segal wrote about the 25,000 soldiers who were held by the Japanese in POW camps during World War II.

"Forced to exist under inhumane conditions, many of them died. Others, however, survived and eventually returned home. There was no reason to believe there was a difference in the stamina of these two groups of soldiers. The survivors, however, were different in one major respect: They confidently expected to be released someday. As described by Robins Readers in *Holding On to Hope*, 'They talked about the kinds of homes they would have, the jobs they would choose, and even described the kind of person they would marry. They drew pictures on the walls to illustrate their dreams. Some even found ways to study subjects related to the kind of career they wanted to pursue.'" (Quoted in Morgan, R. J. 2000, *Nelson's Complete Book of Stories, Illustrations, and Quotes* [electronic edition] 450. Nashville: Thomas Nelson Publishers. From a sermon by Matthew Kratz, *Hoping Against Hope*, 9/3/2011)

For many of us, the difference between life and death – is HOPE.

To offer help in sharing it – Paul didn't only attack what TIM was DOING, he attacked the ROOT of the problem – Tim's THINKING.

Remember: What you know affects what you do. We must KNOW the right things to DO the right things! That is why it is important to remember:

To mature to a grown follower of Jesus, I must learn to see the future through the Word of God – the long view that restores hope when life is hard.

Paul told him (and us) clearly:

- Face your fears.
- Look long and get perspective.
- Take a GOOD LOOK at Jesus – and you will find Him trustworthy.
- Hold tightly on the treasure of God's Word.
- Defend its truth.
- Don't get knocked off course by unfaithful men around you.
- Bathe often in the sweet water of praise.

Lessons in 2 Timothy
Living Hope

Lesson Three: 2 Timothy 2:1-26
"The Anchor"

Have you ever found yourself on a sloped surface that was impossible to stand upright and not slide down? Several years ago, I was cleaning off a slope of some saplings that were growing along the edge of a steep and muddy embankment during a service project. The idea was to cut out all the little saplings, seed the ground with grass seed and spread a type of straw over the muddy banks to give the seedtime to take root without being washed away. I first tried moving horizontally on the slope, but the mud and the slope pulled me down uncontrollably. After a few wide rides downhill, I finally tied myself to a larger tree and moved along the embankment with the anchoring effect of being tied to a fixed station. That seemed to work well.

What about when your life is sliding down a steep embankment of truly depressing issues? How do we anchor to a truly positive and hopeful outlook on life when things appear to be crumbling? Haven't you ever felt like "Grumpy the Dwarf" and you know you aren't right, but you can't seem to find enough to grab onto to keep you from sliding downward?

Long ago, God opened the door in pictures to an anchoring rope of hope that was fixed to the steady tree of spiritual guides – offered in the form of "people pictures."

Key Principle: To gain perspective and a godly attitude, fix your heart on some of the steadying examples that God has provided, and anchor your hope by following their pattern.

When you are in trouble and being pulled downward, you need to pattern as an anchor to a fixed hope – and often that is easier to see in pictures than long descriptions. Paul went into the daily imagery of the Roman home and told Timothy to gain comfort by following the path that people have cut and groomed before him – and it was a great way to help him see truth. Why?

If you have ever gone tromping through woods, lost, and unsure of where your campsite was located, you know the comfort of rediscovering the worn trail. New paths are adventuresome, but old paths bring comfort in the knowledge we are on the right track and can expect to find the place others found before us.

Think back with me for a moment about a guy who was sunk into a cave filled with the stench of human waste and rotting flesh. The time was the first century, and the occupants of the "Mammertine Prison in Roman" were likely joined by an apostle of Jesus Christ, who had been greatly used by God. Facing death, it would be logical to assume the letter we have today about HOPE was an encouragement note written by friends of the condemned man facing death – but the very opposite was true. The letter of Second Timothy is an encouragement note BY THE CONDEMNED to his younger and less experienced friend who was depressed and indecisive. Tim needed hope and inspiration from Paul, who was running out of time to help get Tim back on his feet in ministry. Paul may have lost his freedom, but Tim lost his HOPE – and that is a much worse situation.

Men and women, **we simply cannot survive without hope** – it is as essential over time as food and water. Hopeless people dry up inside and cannot continue the journey. Yet I submit to you that our enemy is wounding many a believer today. We again need to grab the pattern – the proven path – seen in seven examples of workers who were known to Timothy. Fortunately, God doesn't just post expectations – He offers patterns.

First, a word about the Goal.

The text opens with an instruction that is the point of the rest of the reading. Tim's goal was to grow to be strong – not in himself – but in the rich and undeserved supply of God's strength and mercy best pictured in the UNMERITED FAVOR God placed on Tim's life. Paul said it this way:

2 Timothy 2:1 You therefore, my son, be strong in the grace that is in Christ Jesus.

It was the unmistakable goal of God instructed through Paul that Tim grow to full strength and set aside the weakening influence that shame and fear had on his life. His strength was not to be physical, but spiritual, and it was not to be earned, but bestowed. Tim was a dry man that needed to stand under the torrential, drenching rains of God's grace. Favor was freely available, but required abandoning self-trust and works, and deliberately repositioning himself under the constantly renewed deluge of God's love.

Grace is unmerited favor.

We cannot earn it – we have it when we accept it. It is grasping that I do not deserve God's goodness and favor – but in His love, He has decided to give it. It is humbling and de-throning, while at the same time exhilarating... I have a personal beloved relationship with God! It is a gift, but still requires some deliberate action on my part to acknowledge and accept it.

This Greek verb here is actually in the passive voice, so it's more accurately translated, "Let yourself be strengthened" or "be empowered by" God's grace.

Paul tells Timothy, "You won't get strong by drawing from your own strength and working harder at ministry for God!" Don't grit your teeth and push, but open yourself to God's strength, from the grace found in Jesus Christ.

One pastor shared, "Your life for God is like a power tool with an electrical plug. When you're plugged in, God's grace flows through our lives to empower us to do that which we could not do on our own. The love we need to care about people, the patience we need when we're frustrated, the courage we need in the face of fear...all these things come from being plugged into God's grace. Lives that don't plug into God's grace won't have the resources to leave a very significant mark."

Before we look at the people pictures – we need to know there are some GRACE KILLERS.

Clinging to guilt kills the shower of grace. It is still transfixed on our ability and performance to "earn" God's tenderness – and it hasn't really grasped the gift nature of grace. Some people cannot accept God's grace because they **do not think themselves worthy** – and they are right – but that isn't relevant. Grace isn't given to the worthy – it is given to those who place themselves in God's hands and believe His Word knowing they don't deserve it.

Our desire to earn favor equally kills the shower of grace. Years ago, I heard of a professor who taught this in a practical way. I believe it was Charles Stanley that I took this clip from:

"One of my more memorable seminary professors had a practical way of illustrating to his students the concept of grace. At the end of his evangelism course, he would distribute the exam with the caution to read it all the way through before beginning to answer it. This caution was written on the exam as well. As we read the test, it became unquestionably clear to each of us that we had not studied nearly enough. The further we read, the worse it became. About halfway through, audible groans could be heard throughout the lecture hall. On the last page, however, was a note that read, "You have a choice. You can either complete the exam as given or sign your name at the bottom and in so doing receive an A for this assignment." Wow! We sat there stunned. "Was he serious? Just sign it and get an A?" Slowly, the point dawned on us, and one by one we turned in our tests and silently filed out of the room. When I talked with the professor about it afterward, he shared some of the reactions he had received through the years. Some students began to take the exam without reading it all the way through, and they would sweat it out for the entire two hours of class time before reaching the last page. Others read the first two pages, became angry, turned the test in blank, and stormed out of the room without signing it. They never realized what was available, and as a result, they lost out totally. One fellow, however, read the entire test, including the note at the end, but decided to take the exam anyway. He did not want any gifts; he wanted to earn his grade. And he did. He made a C+, but he could easily have had an A.

"Accepting God's favor is part of surrendering our own ability to be good enough. It is never an excuse to become lazy in our walk – only a demand to become realistic in what WE can and cannot do...When we DO RIGHT DEEDS, it is not to be loved by God – it is to honor His undying love for us that was already obtained by grace through faith."

How do we walk in surrender and obedience, all the while basking in the joy of receiving God's grace and growing in His favor? In short, we look at some patterns that make the method clearer:

Seven "People Picture" Patterns to Follow:

Paul showed Tim how people in his everyday life experience exhibited aspects of growing in grace:

First, a Steward (*Par-at-ith'-ay-mee:* "entrust or to place beside or near or set before as in food" – the word for work of "house master, of apprentices"; "teach" is *didasko* – 2:2). This was the most trusted household manager, normally a slave himself, who kept a fine house running smoothly and could be entrusted to take the directives of the owner and see them through. In the later English manor, this position was more that of the butler, or chief steward.

Second, a Soldier (*Stratiotes:*" common foot soldier; soldier in active service" is from "*strateuomai* or "soldier on active campaign" 2:3-4). Roman life intersected soldiers of the Empire all the time, and their singularity offered a picture of one aspect of growing in grace.

Third, an Athlete (*Athleo* – 2:5) was also a common person, many of whom had become celebrities in the time of Paul and Timothy. Roman baths had *gymnasia*, and amphitheaters had practice fields adjacent to them in Rome and Pompeii – along with other places.

Fourth, a Farmer (*Georgos* – *gheh-ore-gos':* "a tiller of the soil, or a vine dresser" 2:6) was also vital to the wine stores and vegetable markets of the ancient Roman city. It is likely Paul had in mind the work of the vinedresser, who was also the wine maker – and avid taster of each cask during preparations.

Fifth, a Workman (*Ergates:* "household or general laborer" 2:14-19) was a part of every large household. Senators at the time of the first century had them by the hundreds, but many Romans had a few. The work done in our homes by machines were performed by household workers – everything from a doorman who allowed people entrance, to the servants that kept the laundry services, etc.

Sixth, a Vessel for God's Glory (*Skeuos:* "household utensils, domestic containers" 2:20-23). Romans loved stuff. Great homes possessed storerooms of vessels. In every sleeping quarter, there was one particular pot that was of vital importance – a chamber pot. Urine was transported to the nearby collection vats for the fullers to use as part of their cleaning ammonia at the local laundry, but it had to be carried in the designated pots that could not be used for other purposes.

Seventh, a Servant (*Doulos*: "household slave, i.e. devoted to another to the disregard of one's own interests" 2:24-26). Slaves abounded in Roman life – but many lived for the promise of getting out from under servitude by buying their way into freedom. The manumission or freeing was common. The household slave was more domestic and clean than the household laborer – who often worked behind the scenes in the gardens and on infrastructure of the home. The *doulos* was the slave most often seen in the home, directed by the householder.

Seven simple snapshots teach how to grow in grace and walk in hope. No single snapshot tells the whole story – but collectively they offer a great set of values and practices.

Picture One: Steward or Householder: (2:2)

2 Timothy 2:2 The things which you have heard from me in the presence of many witnesses, entrust these to faithful men who will be able to teach others also.

The Roman world had artisans, but most of them were trained in apprentice relationships in the home slave system. If the householder you served under believed you were ready to showcase your ability, he assigned to you a "masterpiece" – the one work that would show you were ready to be a journeyman and lead others in work for your master. In Timothy's case, he had as a starting place in training for the world of ministry in the pattern of life he observed in the Apostle Paul himself.

NEVER underestimate the powerful work of quietly walking with God over a long season of life. The example is a blessing to those who see it – whether they admit it or not! When NO marriages last, one quickly believes the institution is unrealistic. When no one walks in sexual purity, it starts to look impossible to do. One of the power trax for teens at the conference I was teaching in was led by a young woman for teenage girls. It was entitled: "Twenty-eight year old virgin!" The point was that it could be done, and there are incredible benefits to following God's Word in purity. How encouraging to a young person whose very education system has largely given up on self-discipline and moral restraint in that area!

At the same time, note that equipping of an apprentice was an understood relationship and an intentional act. This was MORE than just being a good example – this was forming a life intentionally! It had specific parameters and was a defined connection. Where can we see this? Note what Paul told Tim.

First, you heard me teach things – so this wasn't just playing basketball with youth – it included intentional instruction and intense observation.

Second, the lessons were not private – but in front of many other witnesses. There may be others in the room at differing stages of development watching the same example of "how to do it".

Third, they were meant to be passed on. Old practices had value, and new technology would never replace knowing how the whole procedure worked.

Finally, Tim, as the rising leader, needed to be selective about who he should, dedicate passing truth to. That means Paul offered four important thoughts:

- Mentoring is intentional and includes biblical content.
- Mentoring can be in private or group settings.

- Mentoring has as its goal the equipping of the one being mentored so that they would pass it forward to the next generation.
- Mentoring was to be passed to both faithful and able people. The disciple must expect to tailor their schedule to receive – and not expect the mentor to change their schedule to conform to the followers.

Equipping the next generation isn't simply a program. It is a mindset before it is a practice. **It is intentional time spent both in example and instruction that will grow young believers to maturity** – and **mature believers ought to be taking time to be involved doing it on every level of ministry.** Disciples should show themselves to be faithful, and seek someone to pattern them, so they can learn and pass on the things God teaches them!

How exciting that God would shower us with grace and then use us to pour out that grace on others! Paul overtly mentioned at least four generations mentioned here:

- Paul as the <u>Church Planter</u>
- Timothy as the <u>Younger Pastor</u>
- The <u>Disciples</u> of Timothy
- <u>Future Disciples</u> of the group that Tim would reach

Imagine the joy this past week of watching HUNDREDS of young men and women approach an altar to receive Christ. This was not at some powerful band led worship time. It was not a high emotion packed speaking. The greatest response in size was the night a very meticulous presentation of the substitutional atonement of Jesus Christ was spelled out. No fanfare, just truth and prayer – and more than one hundred poured forward to receive the Lord. It was like being in a Wesley revival of long ago. God's grace and the hope of life in Jesus is still drawing young lives by the score!

It wasn't JUST exciting for the students who received Christ. It was exciting to watch many of them who knew Jesus learn how to prayerfully and carefully communicate Christ to others of their generation. Some were learning about Christ in the room – others were learning about SHARING CHRIST by watching someone who really knew how to present the case.

Picture Two: An Enlisted Soldier in Active Service (2:3-4)

2 Timothy 2:3 Suffer hardship with [me], as a good soldier of Christ Jesus. 4 No soldier in active service entangles himself in the affairs of everyday life, so that he may please the one who enlisted him as a soldier.

Paul turned his attention to the Roman soldier – and that was a very common image since they were everywhere in the Empire. The point of Paul's words to Timothy was simple – determine the expectation you have as a follower of Jesus. **In short: endure hardness (2:3). Paul overtly called on Tim to stop asking for a lighter load and work hard for a stronger back!**

Soldiering is an extremely demanding way of life that is designed to discipline every aspect of a soldier's character. They are exposed to the elements, to danger, to times without food or shelter.

U.S. Air Force Captain Scott O'Grady, whose F-16 fighter jet was shot down in Bosnia some years back evaded Bosnian Serb soldiers for six days until his rescue by a Marine Corps search and rescue team – entirely based on his trained of depriving and disciplining himself. He lived by eating bugs and licking the dew from plants. Being a soldier is demanding.

Paul's focus in this passage is not so much on fighting, but on the single-minded self-discipline that remains un-entangled from all but that which would please his commander – Jesus.

One of the most encouraging parts of the coming darkness is that it will separate out the sunshine followers of Jesus. No more will the selfishness of the prosperity doctrine or the compromise of the "positive thinking" doctrine drive the church. The times ahead will force us to choose carefully to stand with Jesus in truth and toughen up. Departure from the Word is making our culture into the most victimized, bullied and powerless generation. Jesus will call us to toughness.

The chief interruption to standing tough in troubling times was not FEAR, but rather DISTRACTION OF DAILY LIFE. Paul reminded Tim that a Roman soldier could not entangle himself in all the affairs of life as a civilian – but lived to please his general. In the patronage system of the period, Tim knew that men counted on their general for salary, retirement and every benefit. They were not to work on the side – but to place their full trust in their general to meet their every need – both then and in the future.

Picture Three: An Athlete (2:5)

2 Timothy 2:5 Also if anyone competes as an athlete, he does not win the prize unless he competes according to the rules.

If being an athlete meant anything in the text, it was the picture of one who learned to discipline his lifestyle AND FOLLOW THE RULES of the contest (2:5). The victorious results come to those who train themselves to walk correctly – both in the game and out of it. An ancient athlete knew that in order to compete in the better games, they had to meet certain requirements – i.e. train for two years before you could qualify to compete.

Apparently, that is still the case. In the magazine *Scientific American* they describe some of the kinds of training Olympic athletes go through: *Training the Olympic Athlete* (6/96). "1,000 hours of intense training will only achieve an improvement of a single percentage point in an athlete's performance. Yet often a single percentage point is the margin of victory in today's Olympic events."

The single greatest point that Paul made to Timothy was this: "Tim, there are rules, and they apply to you as a leader just as much as any other part of the team. You aren't above the rules, and you aren't exempt from them. You will never be what you were called to be making up what is right and wrong by yourself. Ask God – He has a whole book of answers to what He believes is right!"

Growing in grace is not an exemption from walking well – grace is embraced when responsibility to obey is enjoyed and celebrated.

Picture Four: A Tiller of the Soil: (2:6-13)

2 Timothy 2:6 The hard-working farmer ought to be the first to receive his share of the crops. 7 Consider what I say, for the Lord will give you understanding in everything.

Paul moved to the farm – many of which were vineyards tilled by skilled vintners. He pleaded with Tim to see the need for consistent diligence and put every effort into joining the work! Tim needed to gain ownership of the work (2:6). He needed to face the fact that the work may well cost him – it is serious work (2:7-13) and he needed to "own" it day after day.

The words "hard working" refers to work that involves anticipated difficulties, toil, and focus of daily attention. Rising at the crack of dawn and working in the blistering heat until your fingers bleed was not abnormal for one committed to his product. Staggering into your bed at nightfall, only to do the same thing the next day – wasn't light work – ask anyone who does it daily. Farmers from cheese producers to vintners were daily testing their product, adding and changing conditions to meet the demands of the taste, etc.

Great work comes with a price. Keeping a marriage together through years comes with a price. Graduating with your college degree comes with a price. Starting your own business and building it into a successful business comes with a price.

Right in the middle of the metaphors of the work, Paul stopped for a little hymn – an anthem of the Person and work of our Savior!

2 Timothy 2:8 Remember Jesus Christ, risen from the dead, descendant of David, according to my gospel, 9 for which I suffer hardship even to imprisonment as a criminal; but the word of God is not imprisoned. 10 For this reason I endure all things for the sake of those who are chosen, so that they also may obtain the salvation which is in Christ Jesus [and] with [it] eternal glory. 11 It is a trustworthy statement: For if we died with Him, we will also live with Him; 12 if we endure, we will also reign with Him; if we deny Him, He also will deny us; 13 if we are faithless, He remains faithful, for He cannot deny Himself.

"Look carefully at the message of 2:8-13 – Picture your life as being like a wagon wheel. Each spoke on the wheel represents something in your life: your spouse if you're married, your job, your kids, your church, your house and possessions, how you spend your time, and so forth. Where does Jesus fit on the wheel? Is He just another spoke? This text is encouraging us to make Jesus the hub, the source from which all the spokes meet." (Sermon central illustrations)

Here we confront a repeated phrase for the first time in this second letter of Timothy: "trustworthy saying" but we encountered two "trustworthy sayings" in 1Timothy. Most *Bible* scholars believe these trustworthy sayings were songs that were popular in the church at the time. Perhaps some of them were lyrics from worship songs they sang in their worship. This trustworthy saying is a series of **four conditional statements** (2:11-13):

First, the first conditional statement is that if we died with Jesus, we will also live with Jesus. We died when we gave Jesus our life – and the promise to live with Him is one we are focused on more and more with each year of following Him!

Second, the second conditional statement promises that we will reign with Jesus if we endure. The word "endure" is *hupomeno:* the ability to remain under and described Paul's attitude toward his suffering in 2:10. Endurance is remaining under pressure without slipping out. He didn't say if we failed to endure, we would lose salvation – but he did imply we would lose reward – and that is something to consider!

Third, the third conditional statement warns us that Jesus will disown (*arneomai:* to deny) us if we disown him. No true follower of Jesus Christ would betray Jesus. The idea is "to repudiate," and it refers elsewhere in the New Testament to apostasy, or walking in complete denial of things people thought I believed.

Fourth, the last conditional statement is a promise of God's faithfulness even when we are unfaithful (*Apisteo:* not walking in God's view). Now clearly "faithless" doesn't mean "having no faith in Jesus" but rather lacking trust to walk practically in faith's view, even though we still believe.

The promises of following a RISEN SAVIOR are sweet. We should recognize that the days ahead will take work – but not grow long faces about it. Jesus is Alive! He is at work! The culture's darkness will help us see the difference between followers and occasional fans of Jesus! Why the long faces?

"John Bisagno former Pastor of Houston's First Baptist Church tells the story of his coming there to candidate for the position of pastor many years ago. He said that as he entered the auditorium it was dimly lit, with just a few people huddled together. They were singing some old slow funeral type song that was depressing. Later that day he took a walk in downtown Houston and came upon a jewelry store. It was some sort of grand opening and there were bright lights and a greeter at the door to welcome you in with a smile. Inside there was a celebration going on. There were refreshments and people having a good time talking and laughing with each other. They welcomed him and offered him some punch. He said that after attending both the church and the jewelry store, if the jewelry store had offered an invitation, he would have joined the jewelry store!" (Sermon central illustrations)

Picture Five: A Household Laborer (2:14-19)

2 Timothy 2:14 Remind [them] of these things, and solemnly charge [them] in the presence of God not to wrangle about words, which is useless [and leads] to the ruin of the hearers. 15 Be diligent to present yourself approved to God as a workman who does not need to be ashamed, accurately handling the word of truth. 16 But avoid worldly [and] empty chatter, for it will lead to further ungodliness, 17 and their talk will spread like gangrene. Among them are Hymenaeus and Philetus, 18 [men] who have gone astray from the truth saying that the resurrection has already taken place, and they upset the faith of some. 19 Nevertheless, the firm foundation of God stands, having this seal, "The Lord knows those who are His," and, "Everyone who names the name of the Lord is to abstain from wickedness."

Paul told Tim that he would need to see the example of the "Workman" (*Ergates*: "household laborer" 2:14-18). This image may be less familiar to those of us that didn't grow up in a culture where half of our town consisted of slaves and household servants – but the Roman system survived on them.

Household servants bought and brought every item of food into the *domus*, or house. They were ordered by the domestic householder who knew the schedules of each of the house's occupants, and had clothing, food and transportation ready for the master and mistress of the house. Their diligence in every task set reinforced the status of the home – and Romans were VERY CONSCIOUS of status. They were kept on task and hushed from gossip and wasting time as the householder pushed them to keep busy getting tasks accomplished.

Tim was warned to focus on the task of discerning and instructing God's Word – not the enticing rabbit trails of the enemy (2:14-23). Paul knew the enemy would most often use very natural tendencies to sidetrack a worker's enthusiasm. These tendencies include:

- Lazy misinterpretations or understudied inaccurate handling of the Word (2:15)

- Intruding distraction of divisive opinions that must be spotted and avoided in teaching (2:16)

- Jumping on board with the latest "wave" or "craze" that isn't rooted in systematic and thorough teaching of God's Word and leads people to conclusions that either aren't in the Word or openly contradict it (2:17-18). In the case he was dealing with, it was the exploration of allegorical teachings concerning the resurrection.

- Opening the doors to wicked practices would also be prevalent among poor teachers of God's truth (2:19). Instead of teaching people about the lines of God's desire – they would draw new lines in wickedness that God would not have sanctioned.

Picture Six: Domestic Vessels (2:20-23)

2 Timothy 2:20 Now in a large house there are not only gold and silver vessels, but also vessels of wood and of earthenware, and some to honor and some to dishonor. 21 Therefore, if anyone cleanses himself from these [things], he will be a vessel for honor, sanctified, useful to the Master, prepared for every good work. 22 Now flee from youthful lusts and pursue righteousness, faith, love [and] peace, with those who call on the Lord from a pure heart. 23 But refuse foolish and ignorant speculations, knowing that they produce quarrels.

There are no nice ways to describe this section of Scripture but to offer this pointed image. In every home there were cooking pots and chamber pots. Each had their purpose. You couldn't use a cooking pot in a "pinch" for a chamber pot and expect it to still be useful as a cooking utensil – it was dirty. If we want our Master to be able to use us for proper things, we need to withhold our vessel from being used for lusts that defile. If we found ourselves in sin – cleaning was needed for usefulness to be restored.

Picture Seven: A Household Slave (2:24-26)

2 Timothy 2:24 The Lord's bond-servant must not be quarrelsome, but be kind to all, able to teach, patient when wronged, 25 with gentleness correcting those who are in opposition, if perhaps God may grant them repentance leading to the knowledge of the truth, 26 and they may come to their senses [and escape] from the snare of the devil, having been held captive by him to do his will.

A servant that won't listen to the householder will be delivered to the *paterfamilias* – the male head of the Roman home. If they won't listen to him, they can be lashed, beaten, starved or even – in extreme cases – executed. One story from the time of Augustus told of a man who wanted to feed his slave to lampreys in a lake out back for breaking a goblet on the floor by accident.

There was little or no protection for a slave and this word
bondservant is exactly that. Yet, many did passively argue, drag
their feet, spit in the soup and fight the charge of their position.
God's servant cannot act in this way – they must stand for truth,
but not fight in ego. They must be gentle in correction of those in
their care – but not overlook sin.

Here is the point of the lesson in growing in grace and living in HOPE:

- If we follow the pattern of the believers before us who did it well, we will do well.
- If we adjust our expectation to hardship, we will grow in discipline.
- If we will know the rules and play in them, we will have significant victories.
- If we will be diligent to work consistently and hard, we will taste some good fruits of the labor!
- If we will order our priorities, we will be able to set aside distraction for true blessing!
- If we will recall what we are made for, and keep ourselves from defilement, the Master will chose to use us!
- If we won't fight the Master's command, we will be helpful to His cause!

When you cannot figure out how to gain perspective and godly attitude, fix your heart on some of the steadying examples that God provided around you, and anchor your steps by following their pattern.

Lessons in 2 Timothy
Living Hope

Lesson Four: 2 Timothy 3:1-17
"The Life Saver"

The MTS Oceanos was a Greek-owned cruise ship that sank off South Africa's eastern coast on 4 August 1991. According to investigators, the vessel had completed a successful cruise season in South Africa and was now contracted on an eight-month charter from a cruise company out of Johannesburg. The inquiry into her loss revealed the MTS Oceanos was operating unsafely, with loose hull plating, faulty check valves that had been stripped for repair parts and a 10 cm. hole in the "watertight" bulkhead between the generator and sewage tank. These parts were partially responsible for her failure at sea. The vessel only left port the day before she sank. Setting out from the port of East London on the Eastern Cape of South Africa, she was headed north and east toward Durban in Kwazulu-natal, facing into 40-knot winds and 30-foot swelling seas. The normal "sail-away" party on deck was moved indoors due to the rough sea conditions, but most passengers chose to stay in their cabins. The storm worsened and dinner service was all but impossible. By about 9:30 PM local time, the power failed due to a leak in a faulty valve that allowed sea water to back pressure its way into the sewage system. Adrift without power, the crew apparently abandoned ship, but according to the passengers didn't make the announcement to the people on board. As the water steadily rose, the main drainage system backed seawater throughout the ship, spilling out of showers, toilets, and any other sewer connection. Listing to one side and without a crew to assist, British entertainer Moss Hills recognized something was terribly wrong and went to the bridge, only to discover the whole place abandoned. He used the radio to signal an SOS and nearby vessels responded with the South African Navy launching a seven-hour mission airlifting people who could not get to the remaining lifeboats. All 571 people on board were saved – in a rescue organized by an on-board entertainer. Moss Hills, in an interview by ABC News said that he only realized how close they were to perishing when he was lifted off the deck in a harness and brought up to the helicopter. He recalled the sheer relief when he first saw the helicopters coming toward the deck, lowering down rescue personnel to those trapped on the sinking vessel. Everyone loves a good rescue story – after they are safely at home. The problem is we live with a certain amount of daily danger, and the expectation that people will respond to challenges in the best possible way. Sometimes, that is not the case – the Oceanos is case and point.

In the past few lessons from 2 Timothy, we have been following the encouragement of the condemned prisoner, the Apostle Paul, written to a middle-aged pastor who needed to be rescued. He seemed like he was sinking, and the water was rising. Paul wanted to offer him a view of help by setting down the help of seasoned veterans of troubled spiritual seas. Paul's sandals had been wet before – and he knew how to encourage. Yet, any reading of 2 Timothy 3 is liable to get hung up in negative territory. The most cursory reading of the text, at least the first thirteen verses of the seventeen, seem deeply negative. Here is the truth: they aren't. Paul set up the point of his lesson strongly in front of Timothy. He made clear that rough seas were ahead – but that isn't the whole story.

There was a fixed point of hope. There was assurance in the rough sea – it was the steadiness and security of the Scriptures that were tethered to an unchanging God.

Key Principle: Our hope is not in historic moral victories or popular majorities but in timeless truths.

The passage is painfully simple in construction – it has two parts. The first thirteen verses talk about the conditions of the rough seas of humanity ahead. The last few verses shift to

Paul's command for Timothy to respond properly in the face of it all. We can cut the descriptions into two simple words: "them" and "us."

Rough Seas Ahead: A Description of the Non-believer ("THEM" in 2 Timothy 3:1-5a)

2 Timothy 3:1 But realize this, that in the last days difficult times will come. 2 For men will be lovers of self, lovers of money, boastful, arrogant, revilers, disobedient to parents, ungrateful, unholy, 3 unloving, irreconcilable, malicious gossips, without self-control, brutal, haters of good, 4 treacherous, reckless, conceited, lovers of pleasure rather than lovers of God, 5 holding to a form of godliness, although they have denied its power; Avoid such men as these.

Four truths about the sailing ahead:

First, Paul established the timing he referred to:

He says the "last days." Although Paul never wavered in the prison cell, he expressed that he was deeply concerned about the coming trends he observed on the horizon. He knew Tim needed to be made ready, or the current would hit him fiercely and displace his resolve. What time is Paul referring to when he says, "last days?" Is that the "end of time?" That phrase is pregnant with varied meanings.

In one sense, it can generally be applied to the whole period of the church age – which is most of the period between the first and second comings of Christ. In the biblical story, the economy of the "last days" as defined by the prophet Joel could be that broad. It depends on how far away from the chart of time you are looking as to what constitutes "last days." Acts 2 and the coming of the Spirit reminded that the gift of tongues acted as a signal of punishment to the Jewish people in preparation to their serious tribulation and eventual repentance and restoration. The period of "last days" in that view is not the end of time, but the last great economy before God draws Israel back to Himself. It began with the BEGINNING of shame (the tongues experience that followed Christ's departure) and ends with the END of shame (at the return of the Son).

There is a sort of metaphoric use – a picture image. In this way, it can also apply to specific periods of spiritual testing within the church age in specific settings. In other words, some times of persecution and trouble will ebb and flow in history like the waves at the seashore.

It may specifically more intensely apply to the last years preceding our Lord's return to the earth – and certainly does – because the time of "Jacob's trouble" or Great Tribulation will be worse than any previous time.

Jesus reminded us that the beginning of that time is like "labor pains" and the time to follow will be even tougher. (Matthew 24:9).

The bottom line is that we are in the "last days" of the church age, and they will not be completed until the Son of Man steps onto Earth. My optimism concerning my destiny, then, must be in viewing toward Heaven – not in the eventual overtaking of the world by the gospel. The Kingdom will be brought in by the violent turmoil of rebellion and the overpowering of the Savior from His horse of war – not the gentle sweeping of the message to all parts of the earth.

We need to be aware that theological approaches have consequences. If I were to accept St. Augustine's vision of the "City of God," I would believe that no specific time called the "Great Tribulation" will exist in the future, and the rise of the Kingdom of God is coming through the successful movement of the gospel bringing peace and truth to the world. I would believe that the so-called "Millennial Kingdom" was the metaphor for the culmination of the great acceptance of the work of Jesus as King. That sounds like a great future – but I do not believe that is the one set forth in the *Bible* at all. That optimism is based on the church's forward movement and victory – and is very earth-centered. It is held by most Christians in North America today, and it has grown in my lifetime. It is a major feature of the eschatology called "A-millennialism." It sees things getting better and then the Kingdom wins. It sees the difficulties and details in metaphors, and symbols – it refuses the literal reading of the Word as naïve.

From time to time people say to me, "I don't care about eschatology, or 'end times' teaching. It seems far too speculative. I want to be more practical. I am more worried about evangelism." Though I commend them on the desire to reach people – theological underpinning shows in practical work. If I believed that things were going to get better, I would prepare people for trouble with the simple understanding that "in the long run of history" the Kingdom will come by the gospel's victory. Because I am a literalist, I think it will cyclically grow darker and take a battle with the Son from Heaven to break the darkness. I cannot simply prepare you for small waves of reversals – I must prepare the church under my care for a rising tide of anti-God, anti-Christ, anti-*Bible* thinking that will eventually be the world system used to displace RIGHT with WRONG. That may not seem as optimistic – but it IS. It places my hope in ANOTHER WORLD not this one. It places my desire to save the planet as one to save the inhabitants, recognizing the terrain will eventually be taken by a literal FIRE and reshaping. It helps inform the priorities of our work – making us less philanthropic ecologists and more ready evangelists. That view is shrinking, as more and more churches try to bring in the Kingdom of God here and now – and speak less of Heaven. I will not join them – even though I will love them as brothers.

Second, Paul offered words about the character of those days:

He said they will be "difficult days" ahead (*khal-ep-os'*: "hard, harsh, fierce, troublesome, fierce"). It is important to note that not everyone will consider them DIFFICULT. Atheists will have their fifteen minutes of national fame, and agnostics will grow in strength as well. They have seized our schools and made faith look stupid and uneducated, and are now working avidly to seize the hearts of American youth. They have taken control of the airwaves, and much of the government initiatives – and are working to push the church and its influence aside. In our town they are doing it by offering through our tax money a powerful machine that is sweeping even daycare aside into the care of the State. We are systematically being "nannied" into a sheepish population, indoctrinated into political correctness, and having simple terms like "right" and "wrong" redefined just under our noses. The outcome of this will be difficult and harsh on those who believe God has spoken, and that is the condition to which Paul was referring.

Third, Paul referenced the certainty of the coming trouble:

He made clear it will come. *Bible* teacher Ray Prichard tells the story: You've probably heard the old joke about the fellow who was told, "Cheer up. Things could be worse." So he said, "I did as I was told. I cheered up, and sure enough, things got worse."

Fourth, Paul offered the underlying human reason it was coming:

Men will be fully overtaken in redirected inordinate self-interest. Look at the words that define the current beneath the surface, and think of the dozens of news items we could apply to each one of them. They will become:

Lovers of self: *phil-autos*: "love self." Don't lose track of what he is saying here – men have always been deeply selfish. The difference in this time is that such thinking will NOT be considered immature and wrong – but RIGHT and LOGICAL.

Lovers of money: *phil-arguros:* "love shining" (as in coins). The term is not only a lover of COINAGE, but also a lover of the "flashy things." In other words, the day will increasingly yield to the fleeting attraction of whatever is flashing at the moment. The term has within it the notion that people will increasingly lose enduring affection for the LONG TERM VALUES and see the temporal ones as entirely the goal. They will easily trade the savings account for the lottery – because they will LOSE the notion that DELAYED GRATIFICATION is valuable. It has happened with SEX in our culture – where few young people seem to grasp what is LOST in premarital sex – and few adults seem to WANT them to remember that sexual gratification comes at a PRICE.

Boastful: *aladzon:* "empty braggart." Remember, we are referencing what Paul said will replace the biblical worldview's value system. Humility will be seen as a weak force before the "dog eat dog" world of brutes formed by a system that teaches that only the strongest will rise.

Arrogant: *huperephanos: hoop-er-ay'-fan-os:* "appearing above others (conspicuous), i.e. (figuratively) haughty — proud." If you read management books of today, one special piece of advice rises to the surface over and over – you must STICK OUT. Promote the brand of self – that is the essence of this term.

Revilers: *blasphemos:* "slanderous." People who don't think they will answer to a higher power will be emboldened to use the name of the Holy One in blatant profanity. Even more, the vitriol of selfish men will look like the comments section on any "religion" blog by CNN. Read it and you will meet a whole team of the revilers – they are alive a well. *Wikipedia* reports that the articles on Jesus must constantly be reset because of "contributions" from revilers that seek to demean His life and work.

Disobedient to parents: *apeithes*: "noncompliant and unbending." The word for parent is *goneus*, which is from the word "to become!" The term isn't just "disobedient" – that is the tip of the iceberg. It is the word for "apathetic" – totally unmoved by any care for them – as in UNBONDED. They don't think parents should have any special right to shape them – they choose whom they will listen to and follow. They will "become" without regard to their parents.

Ungrateful: *acharistos*: "ungracious; both unpleased and unpleasing." The term "without charity" only touches the surface. The simple idea is ENTITLEMENT. They believe they DESERVE something because they are on the planet. Life is not about making right choices for them – it is about being victimized by the choices of others before them – when they were deserving of so much more!

Unholy: *anosios*: "not walking in an undefiled state from sinful practices and regarding nothing as holy." They won't see LIFE as sacred. They won't see FAMILY as sacred. They won't think RESPECT as sacred. They won't think GOD is sacred – so they will be bold in their decision making on "RIGHT" and "WRONG".

Unloving: a*storgos*: literally "not cherishing;" without natural affection, unsociable (Rom 1:31), inhuman (2 Tim. 3:3 RSV), unloving (2Ti. 3:3 NKJV). The term means, "broken from the God-given bonds of love that once held people together." This will allow them to redefine LUST as LOVE.

Irreconcilable: *aspondo*: "not with contract; unwilling to remain in things not mutually agreed upon; cannot be persuaded to enter into a covenant." The word is so full of modern thinking it is hard to know where to begin. Its simplest meaning is 'doesn't respond to contract obligations.' In business, this is a rampaging truth. I sat with a businessman last week who has contracts where people literally renegotiate shamelessly on the basis that a court case would cost more than settling for less than agreed upon to complete the job! The easy divorce started when Governor Ronald Reagan introduced it in 1969 in California has swept the nation, and now a generation had arisen that simply sees no point to marriage. For the record, former President Reagan later said it was perhaps his worst mistake in office – ever.

Malicious gossips: *diabolos*: "used of devil; false accuser, slanderer." See the news – where we offer a trial of public opinion based on half-truths and non-facts that conform to our preconceived notions of the events – without real knowledge of the events. Much of what is called NEWS today is actually a form of GOSSIP – without sufficient verification and based on bias.

Without self-control: *akrates*: "not operating with dominion." Don't get lost in this! Paul is saying the day will come when people will not think SELF CONTROL is the answer to problems of indulgence. They will argue that abstinence doesn't work and drop that expectation – then begin the process of legalizing things that aid self-control, on the basis that other things are "just as bad" – but missing the point that we are simply reinforcing the value of immediate gratification and the right to always "feel good".

Brutal: *anemeros*: "not tame, savage, fierce." A brutish and savage sound comes from someone who is uncaring about the feelings of those around them.

Haters of good: *aphilagathos:* "not loving good, and despising those who uphold it." Read for one hour the website of Atheist 411 and you will hear how God and His followers are responsible for all the evils of the world. Of course, they make little reference to the regimes of pagans in the recent social past that brutalized populations and needed no god to blame.

Treacherous: *prodotes:* "a betrayer, traitor." The term simply reflected the destruction of loyalty. People will become so self-consumed they will lie, cheat, steal – all because the value of "being instantly and constantly happy" will be their birthright.

Reckless: *propetes:* "to fall forwards, headlong, to be rash, reckless." The term revealed that selfishness and immature thinking will yield the inability to PLAN WELL – since life will be all about TODAY.

Conceited: *tuphoo:* "to raise a smoke, to wrap in a mist; to be puffed up with haughtiness or pride." This idea was that people would grow in SELF IMAGE and see themselves as completing things they haven't actually done. They will have an inordinate ability to see themselves as qualified and deserving, even when they have done little to build a resume of accomplishments.

Lovers of pleasure rather than lovers of God: *fil-ay'-don-os:* "love (hedonistic) pleasures." This one isn't tough – they worship feeling good – all the time, any time and any expense. There is no price too high in society for what will make me explode with pleasure right now! Some will simply call them "addicted to happy", but caution us "don't worry – they can govern well" in spite of this lack of any control in some areas.

Holding: *echo:* "possessing" **a form:** *morphosis:* "shape, resemblance" **of godliness** – denied: *ar-neh'-om-khee:* "act entirely unlike himself" **power:** *dunamis:* "inherent power, power residing in a thing by virtue of its nature." Some will continue to do the things that look like they work, but will not act consistent with the value of those things! God-rejectors will not stop religious practices – just take a consistent position against those who will pose a relationship with God is possible!

We spent a long time looking at that list – because Paul spent a long time making clear what replacing a biblical world view with its competing world system morality will look like. It isn't a reason to despair – because the world's end isn't OUR END. **It isn't GOD'S END. It is MUTINY'S END.**

Still the question remains: "What can I do in the face of the obvious trend to make wrong into right?"

Right Responses Needed: The Responses of the Believer: ("US" in 2 Timothy 3:5b-17)

Mark lines around those who want it both ways:

Don't miss the major thing Paul said in the beginning of this section: The most important thing when entering a minefield is to learn how to AVOID them. That sounds as though Paul is saying **NOT TO ENGAGE** them, but that is **not the truth.** The word AVOID is a specific term that means to **SHUN** (*apotrepo:* "turn away from the mutation they are making" (3:5b).

We don't just try to keep away. We stand up and call false what it is and "connect the dots" between wrong belief and reprehensible practices. We do it to stand for truth. We do it to point out the dangers to those who follow us! During the times of low regard for the truth, we will be forced to RECOGNIZE those who are pulling apart the pattern of Godliness and CALL OUT the truth. We cannot simply let them be called the same as we are – because their mutation is to be quarantined.

This is an example: Recently, the belief blog of CNN again featured the "evangelical" view by **Rachel Held Evans**. Here was a part of her report that I think gives the flavor without betraying her understanding. The article was called: "**Not all religious convictions are written in stone.**"

(CNN) "There's a misconception among many faithful folks that religious convictions, by their very nature, are set in stone. People who change their minds are called flip-floppers or backsliders, accused of capitulating to culture and "conforming to the world." ... In my own life, questions and doubts have served as refining fires that keep my faith hot and alive and bubbling where certainty would only freeze it on the spot. I've changed my mind about a lot of things—the age of the Earth, the reality of climate change, the value of women in church leadership... Like a lot of evangelicals, I grew up in a religious environment that vilified LGBT people. ... Today, I am honored to be the friend of many LGBT people, and I celebrated along with them as Exodus International closed its doors and as the Supreme Court ruled the Defense of Marriage Act unconstitutional. ...In his book *Velvet Elvis*, Rob Bell writes: 'Times change. God doesn't, but times do. We learn and grow, and the world around us shifts, and the Christian faith is alive only when it is listening, morphing, innovating, letting go of whatever has gotten in the way of Jesus, and embracing whatever will help us be more and more the people God wants us to be.'

"A person of conviction is not one who is unyielding to change, but one whose beliefs evolve based on new information, new movements of the Spirit, new biblical insights and, yes, new friends. There's a story in the New Testament about a Roman centurion named Cornelius, whose fear of God and care for the poor was widely known among the people. After receiving a vision from God, Cornelius sends for the apostle Peter, who agrees to meet with him, even though it was forbidden for a Jew to associate with a Gentile. Peter, an observant Jew, had been wrestling with the idea of including Gentiles in the church. But when he encounters the sincere faith of Cornelius, he is moved to declare, "I now realize how true it is that God does not show favoritism but accepts from every nation the one who fears him and does what is right!" He tells the skeptical people who have gathered outside, "God has shown me that I should not call anyone impure or unclean." Peter changed his mind, and the church would never be the same. Despite deeply held religious convictions regarding circumcision and dietary restrictions, he led the way in opening the doors of the church to all who would enter, regardless of ethnicity, gender, socioeconomic status or religious background. We can learn a lot from Peter — not only from his inclusiveness, but also from his willingness to change his mind. Like Peter, God has shown me that I should not call anyone impure or unclean. And that I should not think so highly of myself as to assume I've got this faith thing all figured out."

Let me be clear: Rachel just took the Scriptures about God revealing truth in visions from Heaven and turned them into "convictions" that should be re-framed by "new friendships" that offer reasons to deny what God has clearly said in no uncertain terms in His Word. She is in error in her interpretative method – and, **she is NOT correct about her conclusions from Scripture. She has misused it to teach the opposite of what it said.** Her trusted reference to Rob Bell was a step on her journey to torqueing the Word of God into a different message. Rob has done it by denying hell as the destination of unbelievers, and now she is doing it to allow lifestyle choices that God has clearly defined as abhorrent to Him. I mention it because it is a good illustration of the seriousness of the problem. She represented the EVANGELICAL WORLD on CNN. **I cannot offer evidence that is more potent: Not teaching the proper interpretive devices of Scripture will increasingly allow the *Bible* to be used to wound itself** – even if by well-meaning youths.

Identify those who OPPOSE the truth:

Some of you may be uncomfortable with my naming of Rachel just now. The problem is, I have to name her, and I have to challenge her. When the *Bible*'s clarity is at stake – it is the right thing to do. Look at how Paul handled it:

2 Timothy 3:6 For among them are those who enter into households and captivate weak women weighed down with sins, led on by various impulses, 7 always learning and never able to come to the knowledge of the truth. 8

Just as Jannes and Jambres opposed Moses, so these [men] also oppose the truth, men of depraved mind, rejected in regard to the faith. 9 But they will not make further progress; for their folly will be obvious to all, just as Jannes's and Jambres's folly was also.

The ploy will be to convince the ignorant (and that is most prominently being done among high school and college students today) and allow their voices to challenge the leadership and message of God in a brazen but uninformed way. They have been taught to oppose the truth. They have often unwittingly adopted depravity and rejected God's stated view of right and wrong in favor of another system to evaluate it. If Tim would do his job, people would know the obvious violation. If he compromised, God would have to raise up another to do that work, so that the violation would become more obvious. We must identify where the truth battle lines are being set.

Commit to follow the EXAMPLE of the best who went before us:

2 Timothy 3:10 Now you followed my teaching, conduct, purpose, faith, patience, love, perseverance, 11 persecutions, [and] sufferings, such as happened to me at Antioch, at Iconium [and] at Lystra; what persecutions I endured, and out of them all the Lord rescued me! 12 Indeed, all who desire to live godly in Christ Jesus will be persecuted. 13 But evil men and impostors will proceed [from bad] to worse, deceiving and being deceived.

Paul made the case that Tim watched what God did in and through his ministry as a disciple. He saw Paul handle the brazen and the arrogant. He knew what a mob scene looked like, and knew that rocks and anger wouldn't stop Paul from teaching the truth to a lost world. He saw Paul get pushed around, beat up, and persecuted. Now he heard that WORSE THINGS were ahead. In my view the worse things are brought in by a post-Christian culture. There is a special anger among lost men and women about the moral system we represent. The notions of family, respect, and humility are not only being ignored – they are being vilified in the public forum.

Continue unabated to the COMMITMENT to the Word:

Paul's straightforward words to the flagging commitment of his weakened disciple were unmistakable: Get back to the commitment to God's Word.

2 Timothy 2:14 You, however, continue in the things you have learned and become convinced of, knowing from whom you have learned [them], 15 and that from childhood you have known the sacred writings which are able to give you the wisdom that leads to salvation through faith which is in Christ Jesus. 16 All Scripture is inspired by God and profitable for teaching, for reproof, for correction, for training in righteousness; 17 so that the man of God may be adequate, equipped for every good work.

Being convinced of the Scriptures is not an embarrassment or weakness – it is the source of my strength – as it was for presidents, prime ministers, preachers and peasants for generations. Knowing something is true because the *Bible* says it is, is not small minded or dull – it is taking what my spiritual fathers have known and intentionally applying it yet again to another generation of lost men. It is offering spiritual food to a world starved of truth. In the absence of truth, a starved world will eat garbage. We must give them a choice – because God has already prepared one.

Don't miss that one who soaks in the Word will not be ill-prepared – but equipped for the work ahead! **Our hope is not in historic moral victories or popular majorities.**

Lessons in 2 Timothy
Living Hope

Lesson Five: 2 Timothy 4:1-5
"Four Keys to Unlock a Hopeful Outlook"

Deep inside most of us, there is a desire to hope for better times. Anthropologists tell us that man advanced technologically, largely because he is by nature a hopeful being. It's what drives people to part with money on the LOTTO – the hope that some alignment of the stars or happy fate of God above will bring riches unearned into their pockets. Hope is the song of optimism that God buried deep inside of man that allows him to endure tough times. Yet, for some, the weight of the world has powerfully pushed down their hope, and they admit to a struggle to get back to renewed hope. Even a well-made MOVIE can help us feel hopeful when we are down, can't it? Isn't is funny how we can watch a movie for two hours and be so deeply moved by the courage of the hero or heroine? Did you ever walk out of a movie and feel like you could take on the world, or aliens or zombies or animated Marvel comics characters? I am amazed at the power of the visual medium to awaken deep emotions within us. Did you ever watch a movie in your own living room, and after only an hour, you were crying like a baby when a character that died that you only "met" an hour before? How powerful are the last words of a hero as he lay dying near the end of the movie! Some of those scenes stay with us for years in our mind and heart...

I mention that because one of the things I have always admired about the story of the end of the life of the Apostle Paul is that he ended well. Even as Paul was set aside under guard and then later in prison and nearing the end of his life, he knew how to lift, encourage and instruct. He did desire to become a relic, but rather he wanted his hand-chosen men to push the message forward in his place. He was thinking about the days ahead –

even though he was not going to be a part of them. He wanted to pass the secrets that God had shown him in his years of serving Jesus. He wanted to unlock the hope trapped inside the younger Timothy. He wanted to encourage him – and his letter still does the same for us. It is true that in the background of the chapter, you can hear thunder. Paul foresaw rising troubles and persecution. He knew people were hurting, and it was going to get tough very quickly. With that in mind, he took his experiences of ministry and told Tim how to face the days ahead. He passed on the key concepts that worked well for him, as he wrote under the influence of God's spirit.

Key Principle: Our daily choices make the difference in living out hope.

Paul knew that **people who are effective for God are known for four things:**

- **What They Know:** (2 Timothy 4:1) I belong to Him and I am accountable for this life!
- **What They Communicate:** (2 Timothy 4:2) The truth is found in His Word and I want to live it! I don't want to run around and dabble from place to place looking for the "hottest truth". I want to grow under systematic teaching and learn how to use God's truth in my daily life!
- **What They Refuse:** (2 Timothy 4:3-4) I know my heart will resist truth when it causes discomfort. I refuse to let comfort rule me, and push me to use religion to justify my own wants and desires. I will settle down and stop looking for someone to scratch my ears.
- **What They Focus On:** (2 Timothy 4:5): I will stop avoiding the hard stuff, buckle down and work my gifts to His glory and accomplish God's list for my life.

Let's take a few minutes and break down each of four traits that make a difference:

What They Know: Paul made clear that he knew his real judge is Jesus (4:1).

2 Timothy 4:1 I solemnly charge you in the presence of God and of Christ Jesus, who is to judge the living and the dead, and by His appearing and His kingdom:

He charged Timothy (*diamarturomai: diá*: "thoroughly" and *martýromai*: "witness, testify") using a formula that gave the sound of a courtroom testimony before the ultimate judge – God Himself. What does that mean? In short, the standard of judgment is the standard of the judge. He will mark and grade the lives of the living and the dead. He will bring judgment to believers at the Rapture, and to the nations at the Second Coming. When the Judge enters, the judgment follows.

Why begin the charge - before even making it – with a description of Jesus? Because every believer must be constantly drawn back to one simple truth: you and I work for Jesus. We seek His approval for our deeds.

As a pastor, I know that one of the great traps of ministry is being led by public opinion. It can drive our preaching and teaching, and it can blunt our biblical counsel. People who work in ministry are very often people pleasers at heart. Some have very "political" orientations – to make people at ease and comfortable. That isn't a bad thing, unless it becomes a hindrance to telling the truth. If we recall that Jesus is the only one who actually can judge righteously what we are doing – we will be slower to do what pleases men and women – simply because of their approval. We will talk to Him more, and listen to Him more carefully. We will balance the impulse to make another happy against the insult to God when we make a lie into truth.

At the same time, as believers, we are not to TRY to offend people. Very often, we will be able to help them and we are certain they will feel better when they surrender to the truth of Jesus and His Word. Yet, sometimes we will be an offense because HE is an offense. Try not to cause the offense – but don't shrink when you know you have His holy nod to speak.

Here is the simple principle: I must know I am not MINE. If I believe I am in charge of my own destiny, and can run my own life apart, I am destined to fail God's purpose for me... period.

What They Communicate: Paul called on Tim to communicate the truth of the Word (4:2-4).

2 Timothy 4:2 ...preach the word; be ready in season and out of season; reprove, rebuke, exhort, with great patience and instruction. 3 For the time will come when they will not endure sound doctrine; but wanting to have their ears tickled, they will accumulate for themselves teachers in accordance to their own desires, 4 and will turn away their ears from the truth and will turn aside to myths.

The charge was straightforward to the young pastor – what the world needed was a complete and careful exposure to God's Word. Nothing else would suffice. People need nothing more than God's Word spoken clearly. New methods will rise and fade; gimmicks will dazzle and then flame out by carefully delivered truths which sustain people through all kinds of difficulty and trouble.

How can a believer represent God with boldness? In a word – KNOW the Word. Paul pressed Timothy to be prepared (*yoo-kah'-ee-roce*: or "in season" is "at an opportune time") whether people appeared to be interested in knowing God's Word or not.

The longer I walk this earth, the more I recognize that people do not always know what they need. The bottom line is this: God knows how things work. God shared them, but we are often so easily distracted we don't really listen to what He said. <u>The point is not how willing people appear to hear, but how ready you are</u>

to represent God's Word in a compelling way. They can choose to reject it, but you dare not choose to withhold it, and you dare not be lazy about understanding it. If you say it, make sure it is because you took the time to consider it carefully. Flippant use of the sword can lead to permanent and terrible wounds. We need careful believers who know the difference between their convictions and God's Word. You may believe it fervently, but that doesn't mean God said it clearly. Too often, I am finding believers who know what political affiliation God has, and which immigration plan He supports. We muddy the waters when we take our interpretations and make them the text itself. It is easy to do, and we all have to be careful about it.

We do know for sure the process of giving God's Word to people includes some basic elements:

- **Reprove**: *el-eng'-kho*: "to convince with solid, compelling evidence." **CONVINCE**.
- **Rebuke**: *epitimáō epí*: "suitably on," which intensifies *timáō*: "esteem, place value"; properly, assign value as is fitting the situation, building on the situation to correct. **CORRECT**.
- **Exhort**: *parakaléō*, from *pará*: "close-beside" and *kaléō*: "to call") – properly, "make a call" from being "close-up and personal." It refers to believers offering up evidence that stands up in God's court. Connect with God's big plan and therewith offer **COMFORT**.

Paul also set the stage for later days, and made it clear: the hearer bears profound responsibility in opening his heart to the message of the Word. If people choose to go where the ear is "tickled," they get what they choose. Myths attract attention like the dessert table at the buffet line. Yet, it is meat and potatoes of the Word people will need to endure tough times. Positive thinking and powerful motivational speeches are simply no match to systematically teaching God's Word. **Don't forget: At the center of the work is the Word – or it isn't God's prescribed way of doing things.**

Paul didn't want believers to hide their foundation: (4:2)

Timothy's function in the Body of Messiah was to be a teacher, but every believer is called to model the truth before the world. The command to "preach the Word" includes the verb *kerudzon*: which is to "publicly cry out in order to persuade with." At the same time, the power of the message is multiplied when believer's lives model truth and a positive perspective to life – that will draw people to Jesus!

Paul offered a simple principle: If we lift Him up properly, Jesus will draw men to Himself. If no one wants what we have, we might begin to ask the question, "Do I have a life that reflects who God really is?"

It is easy for us to become unbalanced and portray only "one facet" of God's nature. We can become judgmental and share with everyone that they are "getting what they deserve." Though that may be true, that doesn't express the GRACE of the Lord. At the same time, we may share the love of God with others and never express a frank comment about their agreement with error that is sowing the seeds of their destruction. That isn't God's kind of love - that is sentimentalism. That won't help the person when tragedy strikes and they ask, "Did you see this coming?"

The Word of God includes <u>instruction</u>, <u>correction</u>, and <u>encouragement</u>. It houses truth that cuts me, and truth that heals me. My life should reflect truth in <u>all its facets</u> – and not just one or two.

Go back and look again at Paul's words to Timothy about SEASONS. When Paul said, "Be ready," he used the term *ephistemi,* which means, "to stand upon." The idea was not simply to make sure he was prepared, but rather that he would TAKE HIS STAND on the Word. It is possible that even a man of God could make his stand on his own preferences and opinions.

Never let people turning away from the truth affect your commitment to teaching it.

Paul warned that there would be "seasons" of the truth – times when some tantalizing tidbit would become the focus of the masses. Again, the apostle offered a simple principle: The bigger picture is NOT what is HOT today, but standing with the truth taught broadly and systematically delivered over the longer span will train us to become what we need to be. Fads come and go. They aren't wrong, but they aren't necessary if people are learning the whole context of God's truth. You can chase them, but <u>the temptation will be to become imbalanced</u>.

Don't just know WHAT the tool is for, but HOW to use it:

2 Timothy 4:2b: ...reprove, rebuke, exhort, with great patience and instruction.

Paul knew that God's people must communicate the *Bible* specifically, prophetically, expectantly, patiently and intelligently.

Haddon Robinson, *Making A Difference in Preaching*, p. 93: "In a town many years ago that revolved around the lumber business, the town council decided to hire a new pastor for the town church. One day, the new pastor saw some of his church members dragging logs, which had floated down the river from another village upstream. Each log was marked with the owner's stamp on the end of the log, much like a cattle brand. To his dismay, this pastor saw his church members sawing off the ends of the logs where the owners' stamp appeared. That Sunday the pastor preached a sermon on the commandment, "Thou shalt not steal." After the sermon people said, "Great sermon pastor" and "Mighty fine preaching." But the next week they were back to stealing logs. So the next Sunday the pastor preached the same sermon, but he ended the sermon by saying, "And thou shalt not cut off the end of thy neighbor's logs." When he finished that sermon, they ran him out of town. Now I don't know if that's a true story or not, but it does illustrate the need to communicate the *Bible* specifically."

Paul KNEW where to find truth – but not everyone we know today truly does! We must keep communicating the truth patiently. Paul told Tim to teach "with great patience." Sometimes we can be tempted to give up on people when they don't get it the first time. We can get irritated when people don't respond to a biblical principle the first time they hear about it.

I must be personally careful because too often, we in churches are strong in correcting and rebuking, but weak on patience, so we blast people with guilt. I don't want to use the *Bible* as a club to push people away – and I want to lead them to GOD not GUILT. At the same time, I admit that I am flabbergasted at the way people flaunt sin and disregard truth, and in that shocked state I should remain quiet... but sometimes I don't. While I am confessing, I should also admit that I love chocolate and desert – and rebelliously do not want to eat them in moderation.

Don't forget that we need to communicate the *Bible* intelligently. We communicate the Bible intelligently when we not only show people what the *Bible* means and how it applies, but also why the *Bible* makes the claims that it does. Some people believe that thinking deeply is somehow unspiritual, forgetting that the *Bible* tells us to not only love God with all our hearts but also with all our minds.

I was shopping for illustrations for a teaching I had to do in the first message on Jehu killing off Ahab's family in 2 Kings 9. I found only a few messages on the text I was getting ready to preach, but one particularly intrigued me. A pastor was using the text of 2 Kings 9:20 that says: "The watchman reported, 'He came even to them, and he did not return; and the driving is like the driving of Jehu the son of Nimshi, for he drives furiously.'" He decided to preach on the evils of drunk driving from this text! He evidently thought this was appropriate, but didn't take into consideration that the text had no drinking in it, and that Jehu was fulfilling a mission from God. By that method, I could prove that "furious driving" was actually an act of a godly man on a great mission – the very opposite of the truth he was preaching.

Communicating bits and pieces of the Bible rather than communicating the whole *Bible* intelligently is devastating to our outreach across the country. **We must be committed to communicating the whole *Bible* in its context and in its timeless truths!**

What They Refuse: Paul also knew believers needed to refuse lies in the coming defection (4:3-4).

Look a:gain at 2 Timothy 4 3 For the time will come when they will not endure sound doctrine; but wanting to have their ears tickled, they will accumulate for themselves teachers in accordance to their own desires, 4 and will turn away their ears from the truth and will turn aside to myths.

Robert Withrow in his book, *After Heaven – Spirituality in America Since the 1950's,* offers some alarming statistics:

- 69% of the people in this country do not believe the *Bible* is God's exact word.
- Only 50% of Americans know that Genesis is the first book of the *Bible*.
- Only 33% know that Jesus delivered the "Sermon on the Mount."

It is true: **defection from truth is a reality in our day**. We shouldn't be surprised that error will become very popular – when Paul wrote the "time **will** come." Note he didn't say, "Might come." God chooses His words very carefully.

Defection from truth can be recognized: People "will not endure" is an interesting idea in the original language. After the negative "will not" is the word *anechomai*: "to hold oneself up against, to forbear, suffer." "Sound doctrine" is the phrase that means "healthy instruction." In other words, the time was coming when people would simply **NOT HOLD THEMSELVES ACCOUNTABLE TO TEACHING THAT IS HEALTHY.** (*Hugiaino*: "healthy and wholesome," plus the word *didaskalia*: "instruction or teaching").

Defection from truth has a reason: Note what happens next.

- First, people <u>reject the hearing of the truth</u>.
- Next, they <u>seek out someone who will tell them a LIE</u> that matches their inner desires to do the things that God has said will hurt them and violate His holy plan (*epithumia*: "longing or burning to do that which God has forbidden").

George Barna writes, "To the average American, truth is relative to one's values and circumstances. Only one out of every four adults - and even fewer teenagers - believe that there is such a thing as absolute moral truth." Barna suggests that this disregard for "…truth may be the single most intense threat to the health of the United States and its people." Barna goes on to give the implications of a disregard for the truth: "Without absolute moral truth, there can be no right and wrong. Without right and wrong, there is no such thing as sin. Without sin, there can be no such thing as judgment and no such thing as condemnation. If there is no condemnation, there is no need for a Savior."

Why tell us these things? **God wanted to EXPLAIN the events so that His Word contained a prophetic record.** He didn't leave us in the dark wondering, "Am I following a myth if many or most go the other way?" He told us to SECURE OUR HEARTS in a time when that defection seems huge and rampant. Don't worry! He knew it would come!

What They Focus On: Paul wanted Tim to face the world and do the work (4:5a).

2 Timothy 2:5 But you, be sober in all things, endure hardship…

Sometimes walking with God is difficult because God's people aren't vigilant: *be sober* (*nēphe*: means "un-intoxicated, having clear judgment, enabling someone to be self-controlled") *in all things…* If we let down our guard about controls, we open the flesh to wander, the world to entice, and the devil to drive hooks of guilt into our hearts. Control frees me to serve Christ with my heart! The issue can be simple LAZINESS, but the nature of discipline is that it is harder to maintain when inconsistent. Consistency is the refuge of the disciplined. When the military trains you, they do so by drilling consistency. Do it until you don't have to decide to do it.

What if my daily reading of God's Word was drilled to the point that I just opened the book before I was even half-conscious in the morning?

There are **two issues about our FOCUS** in the verse that needs to be explored.

First, we will be tempted to let frustration cause us to drop our guard – and that will be costly.

Let me put this in Tim's world – that of a pastor – because I know about that world.

The reality of ministry is this: people will often judge pastoral performance based on the response of others – even though we don't control their response. If I preach and ten people get saved, people go away believing that I am doing a better job – when I may have been clearer on another Sunday – but God had a work He wanted to perform today in others through me.

My preparation may not have been better, and my delivery may not have been sharper. **That is why we must keep our focus on one thing: We are to do what we do the best we can – for the honor of the King.** At the same time, the King will use our work as He sees fit. In fact, He may choose to use someone else when we are, in fact, doing a better job – if we use the standards of the Word. By the same token, we may get the fruit of someone else's hard labors.

Our job is faithfulness – His job is the results.

Charles Stanley said it this way:, "God is responsible for the results of our obedience, but we are responsible for the results of our disobedience."

Many believers report a temptation to take frustrations and bury them inside. In moments when we want release from those frustrations, we will be tempted to let down the standard of controls and drop our guard. The enemy, like a boxer, waits for the moment he can land his punch. We need to be diligent and vigilant.

Second, a word about our focus: **We will need to recognize that working with people has always included, and will always include real pain.** In the case of ministry, Paul used the term translated "ENDURE HARDSHIP" is the compound Greek word *kakopathéō* (from *kakós*: "of evil or malicious disposition" and *páthos*: "pain or feeling") – properly, experiencing painful hardship or suffering.

Some things will seem like a "setback" in your life and ministry – but they really aren't. You can't always tell today what God is doing – ministry works like pickling. Brine does its work over time. Don't judge successes or failures too quickly. You cannot opt out of pain if you want to be useful to God in ministry. At the same time, learning to endure is vital to your effectiveness. Don't be too quick to need affirmation in people – nor in circumstances. You and I weren't called to fix things – just represent properly the One who can.

Facing the world meant Tim's job wasn't just inside four walls: (4:5b)

2 Timothy 2:5b ...do the work of an evangelist, fulfill your ministry.

Paul told Timothy that the work INCLUDED outreach. He was to personally do the actions (*ergon*) of an evangelist (one who offers a convincing presentation of the truth of the Gospel). Why did he need to tell him this? Because some go into ministry with an inordinate need to be loved by people. They mean well, but they lead by consensus. In a time of rising persecution – it is natural to stand back and allow outreach to grow quieter. Holy boldness must be prayed for, exercised, and developed. It takes practice, work, and persistence.

The Gospel must be shared. We dare not leave the work for others!

There was a Roman aqueduct at Segovia, Spain, built in 109 CE. For eighteen hundred years, it carried cool water from the mountains to the hot and thirsty city. Nearly sixty generations of men drank from its flow. Then came another generation, a recent one, which said, "This aqueduct is so great a marvel that it ought to be preserved for our children, as a museum piece. We shall relieve it of its centuries-long labor." They did; they laid modern iron pipes. They gave the ancient bricks and mortar a reverent rest. Then the aqueduct began to fall apart. The sun beating on the dry mortar caused it to crumble. The bricks and stone sagged and threatened to fall. **What ages of service could not destroy idleness disintegrated**. (Resource, Sept./Oct., 1992, p. 4.)

Let me encourage you: Carefully plot a direction forward to the goal of serving Jesus with your life.

Paul said it in *2 Timothy 4:5 But you, be sober in all things, endure hardship, do the work of an evangelist, fulfill your ministry.*

Fulfill your ministry:

Paul told Tim to stick to the GOAL God had placed in front of him (*plerophoreo*: "entirely accomplish" your *diakoni*: "area of service"). Tim wanted to CHANGE to something that would feel new and different than the work he had. We all get "antsy" sometimes to move on, because the work of dealing with people is at times arduous. Commitment over the long haul yields the best results. "Short term yardage keeps you in the game, but wastes a lot of time on the clock."

In 1968, Tanzania chose John Stephen Akhwari to represent them in the Mexico City Olympics. Along the way as he ran, he stumbled and fell, severely injuring both his knee and ankle. It was 7 PM and a runner from Ethiopia had won the race. Everyone else had finished and there were only a few thousand spectators left in the huge arena. All of a sudden, a police siren caught every-one's attention. Limping through the gate came 36-year-old Akhwari with his leg wrapped in a bloody bandage. The people cheered. A reporter at the gate asked him the question that was on everyone's mind: "Why continue the race after being so badly injured?" He replied, "My country did not send me 7000 miles to begin a race; they sent me to finish a race."

Paul knew that **people who are effective for God are known for four things:**

First, What They Know: (2 Timothy 4:1)

Do you KNOW you will be accountable for this life to your Master?

Second, What They Communicate: (2 Timothy 4:2)

Do you learn and live the Word of God? Rather than dabbling from issue to issue and place to place looking for the "hottest truth" – are you involved in systematic study to learn how to use God's truth in daily life?

Third, What They Refuse: (2 Timothy 4:3-4)

Will you refuse to let comfort rule you and push to understand truth even when it convicts your life?

Fourth, What They Focus On: (2 Timothy 4:5)

Will you stop avoiding the hard stuff, buckle down and work my gifts to His glory and accomplish God's list for my life?

If you will step up, learn and follow God's Word – you will refuse to be distracted, and your ardent focus will show itself in powerful HOPE. Why?

Because the truth is: Your daily choices make the difference in living out hope.

Lessons in 2 Timothy
Living Hope

Lesson Six: 2 Timothy 4:6-8
"Living in Certainty"

People really are in a hurry today, but I am not sure they really know why! The musical band "Alabama" sang a number of years ago a refrain that captured the thought well. It says: I'm in a hurry to get things done; I rush and rush until life's no fun. All I really gotta do is live and die; But I'm in a hurry and don't know why.

We have to admit it – we live in the days of the frantic rush. I admit it. I am exhausted many nights just trying to keep up – don't you feel that way? I remember one of my friends used to burn frenetically with energy. His mantra was: "I will sleep when I am dead!" The funny part is, as a believer, he knew that wasn't even true. Leaving this body isn't about rest as much as it is about the fascination of a new life in a new location!

One of the things we are all painfully aware of is that the clock is running. We can see it graphically in our morning bathroom mirror. We watch things change around us – sometimes at a break neck pace. We lose dear friends to eternity, and sorrow for our loss even though we know this isn't the end...

Did you ever walk through an old cemetery and look at the epitaphs on the gravestones?

Some time ago, a man was trying to trace his family origin. In the process of his research he visited several cemeteries collecting information from the markers. At one place, he came across a monument with the following inscription: "Pause now stranger, as you pass by; As you are now, so once was I. As I am now, so soon you'll be. Prepare yourself to follow me." Next to the marker, he noticed someone had placed a board with the following words: "To follow you, I'm not content until I know which way you went!"

Isn't that the truth? I wouldn't want to face the end of this life without knowing what was going to happen next. Fortunately, the *Bible* is not silent on the issue. In fact, a hero of church planting and apostleship offered us a great picture of the hope that comes from a secure day beyond the grave. Paul made very clear to the Corinthian believers that God has a future for those who know Him beyond just the physical life:

2 Corinthians 5:1 For we know that if the earthly tent which is our house is torn down, we have a building from God, a house not made with hands, eternal in the heavens. 2 For indeed in this [house] we groan, longing to be clothed with our dwelling from Heaven. 6 Therefore, being always of good courage, and knowing that while we are at home in the body we are absent from the Lord—7 for we walk by faith, not by sight—8 we are of good courage, I say, and prefer rather to be absent from the body and to be at home with the Lord. 9 Therefore we also have as our ambition, whether at home or absent, to be pleasing to Him.

In Paul's letter, he wanted to remind them that here or there, our lives are about pleasing Jesus. At the same time, our walk here is filled with days lived out while MISSING HOME. We live, as followers of Jesus, with the incredible and exciting reality that when we face the grave – MUCH MORE is ahead. Frankly, that makes us really different. Our clock isn't set to the here and now – but to the Master of time. We live here because He has planned that – and we will move on when the trumpet sounds or when God summons us to the divine invitation to graduate from time to eternity…

Key Principle: The hopeful mark of a believer is the statement of CERTAINTY about the future.

Why is that important? Because then truth of our eternity changes the lifestyle of our **NOW**. It is the **ESSENCE** of **CHRISTIAN HOPE.** It is a primary difference between us and the lost world – and it is **SUPPOSED TO BE!**

When Paul wrote the first letter to the Thessalonians, he penned out the earliest letter we have from his quill to this day. He was in his early to mid-forties in age, and he experienced for the first time the move of the Spirit of God in producing an inspired work – destined to be bound in the New Testament to this day. He was writing to those who earlier that year had come to Christ, after a very short time with them in which Paul was forced to move out of town by some troublemakers. The letter has five chapters, and the first three do little but explain what God was personally doing in Paul. Chapters Four and Five are the heart of Paul's teaching, and reflect what God wanted to **characterize believers**. Paul outlined several imperatives:

Believers were to hear and obey God in the use of their body.

1 Thessalonians 4:3 For this is the will of God, your sanctification; [that is], that you abstain from sexual immorality; 4 that each of you know how to possess his own vessel in sanctification and honor.

God wanted the church to be pure in behavior in direct contradistinction to the well-accepted loose living of the brothel filled Roman cities. In the first century, there were more than forty NAMED brothels recalled by writers and historians. **FUN to a believer is living life to please the Savior.**

Believers were to work hard, keep quiet, and focus on caring for people, excelling at other-person centered guardianship of people.

1 Thessalonians 4:10b ... But we urge you, brethren, to excel still more, 11 and to make it your ambition to lead a quiet life and attend to your own business and work with your hands, just as we commanded you, 12so that you will behave properly toward outsiders and not be in any need.

Fulfillment to the believer is experiencing the joy of caring for others – not accumulating more stuff for the estate sale after we are gone.

Believers were to see life and death by new definitions.

Lost people were DEAD (Ephesians 2:1), and saved people who were in the grave were with the Lord in spirit (2 Corinthians 5) but waiting the resurrection of their body in the coming days.

1 Thessalonians 4:13 But we do not want you to be uninformed, brethren, about those who are asleep, so that you will not grieve as do the rest who have no hope. 14 For if we believe that Jesus died and rose again, even so God will bring with Him those who have fallen asleep in Jesus. 15 For this we say to you by the word of the Lord, that we who are alive and remain until the coming of the Lord, will not precede those who have fallen asleep. 16 For the Lord Himself will descend from heaven with a shout, with the voice of [the] archangel and with the trumpet of God, and the dead in Christ will rise first. 17 Then we who are alive and remain will be caught up together with them in the clouds to meet the Lord in the air, and so we shall always be with the Lord. 18 Therefore comfort one another with these words.

The future of believers is Heaven.

Believers, from the very beginning of the spread of Christianity, were to see <u>fun</u>, <u>fulfillment</u>, and <u>future</u> in new ways.

Paul didn't only instruct it – by the end of his life, he **LIVED IT OUT as a model.**

Here is the underlying truth for the believer:

- The clock isn't my Master – the Lord is.
- I walk with a certainty that the world cannot offer.
- We who know Jesus are certain that our life will count for something bigger than our century on this planet.
- We are certain that death is a means of conveyance and not an end.
- We are certain that there is both a purpose to our struggles, and an endpoint to our pain.
- We are certain of a real and intimate communion with our Lord – in a reward that is beyond imagination!

Where did we get these ideas? We got them from the *Bible* in places like 2 Timothy 4:6-8, where I would like to spend a few minutes. Facing death, Paul wrote these words of HOPE to Timothy:

2 Timothy 4:6 For I am already being poured out as a drink offering, and the time of my departure has come. 7 I have fought the good fight, I have finished the course, I have kept the faith; 8 in the future there is laid up for me the crown of righteousness, which the Lord, the righteous Judge, will award to me on that day; and not only to me, but also to all who have loved His appearing.

Can you not hear the HOPE in this man? Paul summarized his life as "I FOUGHT, I FINISHED, and now I have a FANTASTIC FUTURE!"

When I talk to people about preparing for this life's end, sometimes the conversation turns to whether it's a good thing or a bad thing to know in advance that you're dying. There are advantages and disadvantages to either scenario. If you know it is coming soon – you have time to prepare. Many do not like to think about it for so long. They would prefer to simply "drop over" without having to dwell on it. We don't all agree… but if the truth be told—we all know we are dying! The real issue is when not if! Human mortality is 100%. Funny how some of us live as though WE are going to be the exception…

Did you hear about the three guys discussing their obituaries? One asked, "What would you like folks to say at your wake?"

- One of his buddies thought for minute, "I'd like them to say 'He was a great humanitarian who cared about his community.'"
- The fellow who had initiated the conversation replied, "I'd like them to say 'He was a great husband and father who was an example for many to follow.'"
- The two nodded in agreement and looked to the silent buddy. Without hesitation he added, "I'd like them to say 'Look, **he's still breathing**!'"

The text of 2 Timothy was penned by a man who knew his days were severely numbered. He offers us several reasons to look squarely over the edge of death's cliff and see it as a reason for HOPE SPRINGING UP.

Paul argued there are FOUR REASONS a believer has an unstoppable JOY and an overwhelming HOPE:

First, a believer knows his life has more meaning than the century of life on the planet:

Paul said it this way in *1 Timothy 4:6a For I am already being poured out as a drink offering…*

The term to "pour out as a drink offering" is one word in Greek – *spen'-domai:*" to pour out as a libation," i.e. (figuratively) to devote (one's life or blood, as a sacrifice) (spend) — (be ready to) be offered. A priest in the temple would approach the altar of hot coals with a container of wine. As a prayer or special vow was spoken, the wine would be poured on the coals. The wine instantly evaporated giving off a cloud of smoke and a sweet rich fragrance. Even pagan Romans knew about drink offerings. They often ended a meal or banquet with such an offering. It marked the time to rise and move on as well symbolizing the giving of the last drop to the glory of the gods.

That is how Paul viewed his coming death. It is as if he was saying, "*The day is ended; it is time to rise and go; and my life must be poured out as a sacrifice to God.*"

William Barclay remarked, "Paul did not think of himself as going to be executed; he thought of himself as going to offer his life to God. His life was not being taken from him; he was laying it down. Ever since his conversion Paul had offered to God, his money, his scholarship, his strength, his time, the vigor of his body, the acuteness of his mind, the devotion of his passionate heart. Only life itself was left to offer, and gladly Paul was going to lay life down."

You and I who know Jesus have the privilege of consciously pouring out our lives in service to Him by caring for one another, and by reaching those who are so very needy in our world. Some of the needs are physical, and we can serve people practically and help them with temporal needs. Other needs are spiritual – finding God and learning to walk with Him. We can extend a hand to each one, and that is our offering before God. For that, we are not diminished – the impact of our lives grows GREATER with each person we touch. What's more, we didn't start the journey. Many great men and women of God were at it long before us – and it is possible that God has many more generations to follow after us.

My point is this: **We are PART OF SOMETHING BIGGER than just a little club in Sebring.** We are part of God's church – His carefully chosen and blood-bought team to reach in love to a hurting world. We have a vast family that started with the disciples of Jesus from the Gospels, and has grown in number until now. Don't let the world try to tell you that no one is left in our family. God has thousands upon thousands He has called to be a part of what we are doing.

- In a small village in Africa today, there is a huddled group who trust Jesus, and want to serve Him with their whole heart.
- We see them in Cambodia, where rural villages are being touched with the Gospel.
- Hiding inside during curfew in Cairo are small groups of Christians who are reading God's Word and learning to trust Him for the days ahead.
- On and on it goes - Syria, Afghanistan, Iraq, Ireland, Italy, Mexico.

Pick a nation and God is at work in some place that CNN will never go... and YOU are a part of it all!

Second, as a follower of Jesus, I know physical death is a means of conveyance, not an end.

Paul said it this way in *2 Timothy 4:6b ...and the time of my departure has come.*

The word "departure" is *analusis*. That word had at least **four discernible usages**:

- It was used as a **Nautical Term**. This was a term sailors used for the un-mooring of a ship. When a ship would set sail, and move out of the harbor, people would stand on the pier and watch the vessel move toward the horizon. He was at the quay, ready to go.

- The term had a **Military Use**. When soldiers would fold up their tent and move on to another campaign, the taking down and folding of the tent invited the use of the same word. <u>He was being folded up and readied for a new place.</u>

- There was a **Political Use**. The term was sometimes used for the release of a prisoner from bonds. <u>He was being loosed from the constraints of the warfare this side of Heaven.</u> You see, our brothers and sisters who have gone home to Jesus are not only free from pain – they are free from their own SIN NATURE! Their ego is completely God-tempered!

- There was an **Agricultural Use**. When a farmer unburdened the ox and removed the yoke it was a kind of "loosing" that was also covered by this word. The fact is, <u>the ministry burdens of Paul were about to be removed from his shoulders.</u> Death was not his penalty; it was his relief. If you have even sat with one who was suffering, you know the feeling very well.

In Hollywood, there are those who know how to make an entrance... **I want you to KNOW HOW TO MAKE AN EXIT!** When we leave this body, we sail away to another port. We pull up the tent pegs. We are a prisoner set free. We lay down the burden of this fallen physical life. We go home with God – untethered, unbound, finally tasting our promised freedom! This is another HOPE BUILDER the Negro spiritual songwriter reminded us with: "Free at last, free at last, thank God Almighty I am free at last!"

Third, a believer knows that life's struggles are not in vain – and they have a soon-coming end.

Paul said it this way: *2 Timothy 4:7 ...I have fought the good fight, I have finished the course, I have kept the faith.*

Paul was able to face his departure from this life with confidence because he knew he had successfully "finished his race" (v. 7). Paul looked back to the past and said, "My life has not been easy, but it has been worth it." Look at the realism of Paul's eyes on his history. He used **three word pictures from the athletic world to make his point:**

- **I have fought the good fight.**

The term "FOUGHT" is *agonizomai*: a descriptive word for a struggle contending with an adversary for the prize. We get the term "agonize" from this word! Romans had both wrestling and a crude form of boxing in their day.

The truth that seems to escape some of the "prosperity people" is that not only can life be tough, but after the Fall the battle is inevitable. The world doesn't play fair. The devil has no interest in being gentle. The flesh rages against what is right within. **Sometimes we must do hand-to-hand, down and dirty combat with each. It's truly a fight, but finishing well is worth the effort.** The struggles will honor the Master – and nothing will be more important when we stand before Him!

- **I have finished the race.**

The verb *teleo* means "to end or come to the point." In commerce, it was a word for "completed" or "paid in full." In athletics, it was a racing term for a long race – like a marathon. **Finishing meant, in this case, simply not giving up.** Paul gives to believers a view from near the finish line. He's nearing his big finish in life's arduous marathon and offers to his younger protégé, an encouragement. He said, "Tim, let me tell you how I feel right now, just yards from the end. There is a burst of satisfaction that I've got going on inside me as I approach the finish line." Here was a coach calling the play with seconds left on the game clock, and down by two – but with a great line! You can hear Paul telling Tim – "Finish the game! It isn't over! Go for it and leave it all on the field!" That is where the satisfaction comes from. The half-hearted warrior knows the ordeal – the persistent one knows the satisfaction.

- **I have kept the faith.**

Paul looked at his own record, and concluded with joy that he had run by the rules. He hadn't cheated, cut corners, or covered over his bad performance.

This is similar to the thought of *1 Corinthians 9:24-27, Do you not know that in a race all the runners run, but only one gets the prize? Run in such a way as to get the prize ...Therefore I do not run like a man running aimlessly; I do not fight like a man beating the air. No, I beat my body and make it my slave so that after I have preached to others, I myself will not be disqualified for the prize.*

One commentator (William Barclay) writes: "The one thing necessary for life is staying power, and that is what so many people lack.

"A very famous man was offered a writer to help him complete his biography while he was still alive. He refused to move on the project, for he reasoned: "I have seen far too many men fall out on the last lap."

Paul could see the end; he knew he kept the faith. He did it by staying close to Jesus and living INTENTIONALLY inside the Word. **He stayed at it until it was done right!** He had taken no short cuts, and avoided no obstacles. He ran from no conflict – but faced the problems and opponents head on. Instead of circumventing the mountains, he climbed them. He weathered the storms faithfully. Moses prayed for God to *teach us to number our days, that we may apply our hearts to wisdom* (Psalm 90:12). Paul did that. We can too.

Fourth, a believer awaits a stunning reward – and we didn't earn it.

Paul said it this way: *2 Timothy 4:8 In the future there is laid up for me the crown of righteousness, which the Lord, the righteous Judge, will award to me on that day; and not only to me, but also to all who have loved His appearing.*

Paul looked toward his future and in essence said, "I can't wait." He looked forward to his reward, "*a crown of righteousness*" (*stephanos*: "a VICTOR crown") used at competition and completion in sport contests. These were the laurel wreaths of the ancient Olympic style games – long before GOLD MEDALS were offered. The wreath had little intrinsic value – its worth came from the occasion and the hand that placed it atop the head of the victor.

...the Lord, the righteous Judge, will award... has an accompanying word in Greek, *monon*: "merely — alone, but, only." Paul knows the ONLY real judge of this life is his Master, Jesus.

Heaven is not first about gates of pearl and golden streets. It is about the presence of the Lord. Jesus said, *I go to prepare a place for you that where I am there you may be with me.* For the lover of God the presence of God is the ultimate reward.

In one of his books, A.M. Hunter, the New Testament scholar, related a story of a dying man who asked his Christian doctor to tell him something about the place to which he was going. As the doctor fumbled for a reply, he heard a scratching at the door, and he had his answer. "Do you hear that?" he asked his patient. "It's my dog. I left him downstairs, but he has grown impatient, and has come up and hears my voice. He has no notion what is inside this door, but he knows that I am here. Now then, isn't it the same with you? Even though you don't know or understand everything that's on the other side, you know Who is there. That's what makes the difference."

Paul Azinger was a graduate of Brevard Junior College in Brevard County Florida. He went on to FSU before he turned pro as a golfer in 1981. He was named the PGA player of the year in 1987. Six years later, he won the coveted PGA championship (1993). At the age of 33 he had a remarkable ten tournament victories to his credit. The very next year Azinger was diagnosed with cancer. He wrote of his experience. "A feeling of fear came over me. I could die from cancer. Then another reality hit me. I'm going to die anyway, whether from cancer or something else. It's just a question of when. Golf suddenly became meaningless to me. All I wanted to do was live." As Azinger faced the possibility of his own death, he remembered something that Larry Moody, a chaplain to the pro golfers, had said to him. "**Zinger, we're not in the land of the living going to the land of the dying. We're in the land of the dying trying to get to the land of the living**." Azinger beat the cancer. He recovered from chemotherapy and returned to the PGA tour, but Job's question: "If a man dies, shall he live again?" (Job 14:14) changed his life. Azinger wrote, "I've made a lot of money since I've been on the tour. I've won a lot of tournaments. But that happiness is always temporary. The only way I have ever found true contentment is in my personal relationship with Jesus Christ. I'm not saying that nothing ever bothers me and I don't have problems, but now I've found the answer—the answer to the six-foot hole."

Paul said it already in this letter, but in different words: *...I know whom I have believed, and am convinced that he is able to guard what I have entrusted to him for that day (2 Timothy 1:12).*

Matthew Huffman was the six-year-old son of missionaries in Brazil. One morning he began to complain of a fever. As his temperature climbed, he began to lose his eyesight. His mother and father knew he needed medical attention so they placed him in the car and rushed to the hospital. As they were driving, Matthew was lying on his mother's lap, and began to do something his parents will never forget. He extended his hand in the air. When his mother took it, he pulled it away and extended it again. Once again, she took it and again he pulled it back and reached into the air. Confused, the mother asked her son, "What are you reaching for, Matthew?" Matthew responded, "I'm reaching for Jesus' hand." And with those words, he closed his eyes and slipped into a coma from which he never would awaken. He died two days later, a victim of bacterial meningitis. In six years of life, Matthew learned the one lesson no one can afford to miss in this life... **know what the end is all about!**

Friends:

- **Death is Inevitable.**

Hebrews 9:27: And as it is appointed unto men once to die, but after this the judgment.

In order to live a life without regrets, we need to know what to live for. The world has it all wrong. They say you only live once so go ahead and grab all the gusto you can. Party hard, live loose because when you die, that's it. That philosophy teaches that the only thing to live for is immediate satisfaction and gratification. It teaches that the highest purpose in life is to be happy and pain free. But the Bible paints a very different picture of life. In fact, we are warned not to love this world or the things in this world.

- **Death is impartial.**

It is no respecter of persons. The old will die; some young will die. To live a life of no regrets, we must learn what is important in life. We have to learn to trade monuments of man's achievements for moments in God's presence. There is a place where all this world's goods will lose their luster. Paul lived with no regrets because he kept eternity in view.

- **Death is often unexpected.**

We make material preparation (buy a good insurance benefit for the surviving relatives and sometimes buy a nice burial ground) but we must make a spiritual preparation! Death need not be a mystery or a loss!

1 CORINTHIANS 15:54 But when this perishable will have put on the imperishable, and this mortal will have put on immortality, then will come about the saying that is written, "Death is swallowed up in victory...."

I want to read again our short text for this lesson, but I want you to hear it in another translation – a paraphrase called *The Message:*

"You take over. I'm about to die, my life an offering on God's altar. This is the only race worth running. I've run hard right to the finish, believed all the way. All that's left now is the shouting – God's applause! Depend on it; He's an honest judge. He'll do right not only by me, but by everyone eager for His coming." 2 Timothy 4:6-8 (paraphrase Randall D. Smith)

Do you possess the hope that comes with Christian CERTAINTY? IF NOT, WHY NOT?

Paul used this language about death.

Philippians 1:20-24: I eagerly expect and hope that I will in no way be ashamed, but will have sufficient courage so that now as always Christ will be exalted in my body, whether by life or by death. For to me, to live is Christ and to die is gain. If I am to go on living in the body, this will mean fruitful labor for me. Yet what shall I choose? I do not know! I am torn between the two: I desire to depart and be with Christ, which is better by far; but it is more necessary for you that I remain in the body."

For to me, to live is Christ and to die is gain. What does that mean?

First, it means that God has a purpose for us in this life – to walk with Christ. We are not floating on a rubber raft in the ocean with nowhere to go and no reason to be there.

Life has been described as propping a ladder against a wall, and spending all your years climbing it. Too many people will climb all their lives, only to get to the top and realize they were climbing the wrong wall.

Second, it means that in death a believer gains something. What is that?

- We gain a **better body** – a glorified, immortalized, resurrected body. 1 Corinthians 15 says that in this present body of clay we're subject to all the sorrows and tears that life deals out. Age, sickness, and finally death are the inevitable end of this house made of the dust of the Earth. But in death and the resurrection we gain a better body, one that can never grow old, know disease, suffer pain, and can never die. No more cough, no more cancer, and no more consumption. We gain a better body.

- We gain a **better home** – John 14 reminds us that Jesus is preparing the next dwelling for us! Paul is able to face his departure from this life with confidence because he knew where he was headed. His departure from here means his arrival in Heaven. Paul knew without a shadow of a doubt where he was headed in eternity.

Do you?

Paul says in *1 Corinthians (5:6, 8) Therefore we are always confident, knowing that while we are at home in the body we are absent from the Lord... (8) We are confident, yes well pleased rather to absent from the body and to be present with the Lord.*

Do you realize that the Bible says that you can know for sure where you are headed in eternity?

1 John 5:13, says These things I have written to you who believe in the name of the Son of God, that you may know that you have eternal life. (NKJV)

Death does not have to be a leap into darkness into the great unknown.

"So, like a prisoner awaiting his release, like a schoolboy when the end of term is near, like a migratory bird ready to fly south, like a patient in the hospital anxiously scanning the doctor's face to see whether a discharge may be expected, I long to be gone – extricating myself form the flesh I have too long inhabited, seeing the great doors of eternity swing open ... – such is the prospect of death for a Christian." (George Sweeting, *Can I Die Well? Moody Monthly*, Jan/Feb 2003, p.70)

- We gain a **better inheritance** – Ephesians 1-3 reminds us that the believer's place and reward is not here – it is in Heaven. Living for God on Earth has its advantages now – a clean conscience, freedom, purpose, meaning, hope. But the full value of the Christian life will be seen in Heaven.

- We gain a **better fellowship** with Jesus – the Christian life on Earth was one of faith, believing before seeing, but Heaven works differently, for we see the Lord face to face.

I'm Free

Don't grieve for me, for now I'm free;
I'm following the path God has laid, you see.
I took His hand when I heard him call;
I turned my back and left it all.
I could not stay another day to laugh,
to love, to work, to play.
Tasks left undone must stay that way;
I found that peace at the close of day.
If my parting has left a void,
then fill it with remembered joy.
A friendship shared - a laugh, a kiss,
Oh yes, these things I too will miss.
Be not burdened with times of sorrow,
I wish you the sunshine of tomorrow.
My life's been full; I savored much, Good friends,
good times, a loved one's touch.
Perhaps my time seemed all too brief.
Don't lengthen it now with undue grief.
Lift up your hearts and peace to thee,
God wanted me now;
He set me free.

Unknown

The hopeful mark of a believer is the statement of CERTAINTY about the future.

Lessons in 2 Timothy
Living Hope

Lesson Seven: 2 Timothy 4:9-22
"Undistracted"

When she called us, her voice was broken – a reflection of her broken heart. There is no pain like the searing burn of the loss of a child. A simple picnic and a happy family time were forever stained with painful loss. She was setting the picnic table, and he was grilling the burgers. For only a few minutes, they lost track of the toddler. When they realized he had wandered, they both felt the flash of pain and a sick feeling, as they dropped what was in their hands and ran down toward the pond a hundred steps off the back patio. Seeing her child face down in the water was more than she could bear. He charged into the shallow pond, but it was too late – and now their hearts were broken. Guilt swept through the hole in their hearts. How could they have lost track of their child? How could they comfort each other and face the days ahead? How could they keep their other two children safe without smothering them? These were the painful pressures they felt – and they all came at one time.

First, there were the EMTs and their horrified looks. Then there was the police officer who seemed to lack the compassion one needed for such a delicate task of asking questions to dazed and bruised hearts. Finally, there was the trip to the hospital, then to the funeral home. Questions were pelted by family members, clueless friends tossed platitudes, but they were barely holding it together – and that is when she called.

Regardless of how you feel about the inattention this young couple gave to their child, you and I have to admit the obvious – anyone can get distracted. No one is insulated from making a critical mistake when operating a motor vehicle or watching a child. Focus is critical in a world full of distractions. Add to that the fact that most of us have been duped into believing that our brain can multi-task – like a dual core processor – and the tendency to be distracted can bring us into certain peril.

Distraction isn't only an issue when it comes to SAFETY, but also to SPIRITUAL GROWTH. The simplicity and passion of our early walk in the Word, our relationships to people, and our intimacy with God can easily get lost in the barrage of other "Christian agenda items" (like service, programs, property management, etc.) The issues of life are demanding, and it takes fervent and deliberate focus on the most important issues to keep us walking with God through the mess of daily living.

I want to take us back to a simpler faith – and the place to look is the end of the last letter of Paul's writings in the New Testament – the last part of 2 Timothy 4. Paul was facing his own end on Earth, and it was clear that his magnificent career as a writer of the Word given by the Spirit of God was coming down to its final word.

His career as a writer spanned twenty to twenty five years. It grew in four stages: Prophetic, Polemic, Philosophical and Pastoral. By the end, Paul settled into the idea that ministry is not just about the future, not just about being correct, not just about understanding who you are in Christ and grasping great heavenly truths – it is about friends and cloaks when you get cold.

Key Principle: God's best work is accomplished in followers who learn to focus on the three eternal parts of life: people, the Word and intimacy with God.

Go back with me to the dank and putrid dungeon, and listen as the seconds tick away in the final moments of Paul's life. **What did he learn?**

Focus on People:

Paul learned, through his tough but fruitful ministry, that a life lived serving God is all about PEOPLE. He did not subscribe to some MONASTIC view of holiness that moves the believer from the fray of everyday living. Rather, he made life about a series of people – different types – that he experienced, and now he wanted to "turn the light on" for Timothy.

One of the mistakes of youth can be seen in their handling of people. As teens, we all pass through a time when we don't recognize the wisdom of those who love us the most, and many of us fell prey to peers that had little more wisdom than we did – but perhaps had more "street smarts." Learning to read people and growing in our ability to work together with people is a key to our success in life, and in the ministry of service to one another. Listen to what Paul wrote to the younger pastor…

2 Timothy 4:9 Make every effort to come to me soon; 10 for Demas, having loved this present world, has deserted me and gone to Thessalonica; Crescens has gone to Galatia, Titus to Dalmatia. 11 Only Luke is with me. Pick up Mark and bring him with you, for he is useful to me for service. 12 But Tychicus I have sent to Ephesus. …14 Alexander the coppersmith did me much harm; the Lord will repay him according to his deeds. 15 Be on guard against him yourself, for he vigorously opposed our teaching. 16 At my first defense no one supported me, but all deserted me; may it not be counted against them… 19 Greet Prisca and Aquila, and the household of Onesiphorus. 20 Erastus remained at Corinth, but Trophimus I left sick at Miletus. 21 Make every effort to come before winter. Eubulus greets you, also Pudens and Linus and Claudia and all the brethren. 22 The Lord be with your spirit. Grace be with you.

In his closing remarks, Paul offered to Timothy what looks like a shopping list of sixteen names. **Read the end of the book** quickly, and it sounds like a roster for a baseball team, or roll call in a college classroom: Demas, Crescens, Titus, Like, Mark, Tychichus, Alexander, Prisca, Aquila, Onesiphorus, Erastus, Trophimus, Eubulus, Pudens, Linus, Claudia. Obviously, Paul was wrapping up the letter with a few comments to Tim about what he had done in relation to the team of people that were a familiar part of first century church ministry.

A closer look at the name list reveals two things:

- **Paul's had a variety of relationships that were very important to him in the handling of the message of Jesus – his work was among and about PEOPLE.** His end comments were not simple administration – they were of the work of co-laborers and fellow servants.

- **Paul saw great value in all of the other people in the ministry – though many had relatively minor contributions compared to the Apostle.** We don't know much about most of the people on the list. There was no great council of the church called by Eubulus, and there is almost nothing known about many of the other names listed in the text – but Paul recalled them and God recorded them. The reason is clear: Anyone who yields himself to the power of God's transforming work can begin to see that God can accomplish great things through the smallest among us. No man can offer another a true measure. Our work is rightly measured by our Master alone.

Make sure people know they are important.

Look at the beginning of the portion, back in verse nine. Paul opened with an "I need you – please come soon" (4:9) request. The beginning of a focus on people is a genuine recognition of our NEED for what others bring to our lives and to the work of the Savior. We cannot really minister in the lives of others until we believe that we not only have truth to offer THEM in terms of a relationship with God, but they have VALUE to God regardless of their current state in regards to a walk with Him. People are loved by God, even when they are resisting Him, and don't see the value of having HIM in their daily lives. We need to see the value, or we will blow the opportunity to be used of God in their lives.

Our Daily Bread offered a great illustration of this: "A story is told of a man who loved old books. He met an acquaintance who had just thrown away a *Bible* that had been stored in the attic of his ancestral home for generations. 'I couldn't read it,' the friend explained. 'Somebody named Guten-something had printed it.' 'Not Gutenberg!' the booklover exclaimed in horror. 'That *Bible* was one of the first books ever printed. Why, a copy just sold for over two million dollars!' His friend was unimpressed. 'Mine wouldn't have brought a dollar. Some fellow named Martin Luther had scribbled all over it in German.'" (*Our Daily Bread,* June 7, 1994)

Here is the truth: we won't long to reach people when we don't LOVE people and VALUE people. We will see them as a hassle, and not as a wonder made by God. One of the ways to practice seeing the value of people is rehearsing in our minds when they can TEACH US about life. We have things to LEARN from others, and in opening ourselves to learning, we help communicate the value of the other people and make a real life connection.

Paul did that, and the request reflected that he knew he had need of Timothy HIMSELF – not just things Tim could bring to him in prison. The sense of loneliness Paul felt could be eased by Tim's presence.

Don't forget that many people, like Tim, probably didn't see their own value. Up against the intellect, the capability, the accomplishments of Paul – they felt small. For those among us who have lived lives of success, who have accomplished great feats for God – it is especially important for that kind of person to work hard to show value in the others around them. I have served with some great men. Pastor Vince, before he went to Jesus, served in Africa for many years. His last classes alone brought literally hundreds to Jesus Christ. Yet, he never made people feel small. He treated me with respect and kindness, even though my life hadn't come close to his in accomplishments for the King.

Recognize there are a variety of people in your life.

Beginning a closer study at verse 10, I felt it may be helpful to move the people from the list into groups that reflected what "faced his own death. I believe the text exposes **eight types of people:**

Let me start with those who were a negative influence on Paul – to get past the bad news and into the good:

Defectors:

Quickly jumping off the page in 2 Timothy 4:10 is **Demas** who felt the connection to the world more deeply than the connection with me (4:10a). He was a former companion of Paul and left Paul – drawn away by the things of the world.

Who hasn't seen this? In the life of our family, I have watched my parents, my brothers and sisters, and even my wife and me, draw close to help some individuals that take from us, but don't really follow Jesus. They start off looking like they want Jesus, but after a while, the world's attractions draw them away. The more you gave, the harder it is to let go without pain.

Here is the truth, that I will call the **Defection Principle:** We will invest time and energy in some who will slip away, attracted by other priorities.

In Matthew 13 Jesus encountered the same thing! In the background, there were people leaving the ministry, and pressure was coming on Jesus to "get the crowds back." He offered **a step parable, where each thought was built on the previous thought:**

- **The Sower on the Terrace** (Mt. 13:3-9; 18-23): The problem with followers is not the seed, but the soil. The sower is true, the seed is good, but the soil must be right to get growth.
- **The Wheat and the Tares** (Mt. 13:24-30; 36-43): Some leave us because they were never truly with us.
- **The Mustard Seed** (Mt. 13:31-32): Some leave because they do not understand my priorities!
- **The Leaven** (Mt. 13:33): The Kingdom WILL have its effect – no need to worry.
- **The Treasure** (Mt. 13:44): Some have left but they are making preparation to take it fully!
- **The Pearl** (Mt. 13:45-46): Some will be coming that have left all behind to grasp it!
- **The Dragnet** (Mt. 13:47-50): It is the nature of the Kingdom to grab all kinds – and LATER it will be sorted out who was the true follower.

Not only will we have people that seem to be with us and then show themselves to be of another mind, but the fight for the hearts of men is a SPIRITUAL battle – and as such, it will bring us into conflict. Drop your eyes down to verse 14 for the second kind of person.

Enemies:

Alexander the Coppersmith set out to harm Paul (perhaps by testifying against him in addition to standing against Paul's teaching) – but Paul had to leave him to the Lord's judgment and warn Tim to keep an eye out for him (4:14-15). Paul had no illusions that enemies existed. He had gone out into a spiritual war, and he raised the eyes of the enemy and his minions. Paul had previously instructed the church in Ephesus 6:10-20

(Call/Conduct/Conflict) that there were battle armaments: belt of truthfulness, breast plate of right choices, sandal cleats of the identity in Christ, then as necessary – the blocking and locking shield of faith, the helmet of salvation, and the small dagger of the *rhema* Word. All were to be used with constant prayer and watchfulness. Paul was very conscious that he was at war.

I often find that believers walk without a consciousness that there is an enemy crouched in the tall grass of life. He is seeking to destroy and uses people to get that destruction to tumble onto us. Paul didn't hate people – but he also didn't underestimate how much damage people could do when operating as stooges for the underworld. He didn't HATE them, because he knew that would hurt his own walk.

Dale Carnegie wrote: "When we hate our enemies we give them power over us – power over our sleep, our appetites and our happiness. They would dance with joy if they knew how much they were worrying us. Our hate is not hurting them at all, but it is turning our days and our nights – drawing us into hellish turmoil."

God offered encouragement in the war in the past when he wrote things like – Isaiah 43:2: *When you pass through the waters, I will be with you; and when you pass through the rivers, they will not sweep over you. When you walk through the fire, you will not be destroyed; the flames will not consume you.* (Randall D Smith paraphrase)

Don't misunderstand that as a blanket promise that life won't hurt – that isn't the context. What God consistently told His people is this: "Follow Me and I will lead you through life to complete your call!"

Let me offer this **Attack Principle:** Some will attack us and try to destroy what we are building as we reach out for the Lord – and that was promised from the beginning.

Jesus made the promise in Matthew 5:11 Blessed are you when [people] insult you and persecute you, and falsely say all kinds of evil against you because of Me. 12 Rejoice and be glad, for your reward in heaven is great; for in the same way they persecuted the prophets who were before you.

We must be wise and keep our eyes open, but not walk around with a chip on our shoulder! We pass the names of those who oppose the Gospel, not as an act of hatred, but in an attempt to protect those who come behind us by making them aware of potential deceptions. We needn't get paranoid, but we don't want to be ignorant of the enemy's schemes and devices.

Now let me turn to the many people that were positive in the life and heart of Paul:

Vision Expanders:

Paul moved his attention from warning Tim, to celebration of his co-workers. He said the gospel was moving forward with **Crescens** in Galatia and **Titus** in Dalmatia – both out doing the work (4:10b).

I love to hang out with missionaries who are actively on the battle lines around the world. They are people under fire, but they are people who have their blood pressure heightened and their mind sharpened – because they are in the midst of the fight. The pressure of the front line has toughened their resolve, and the daily need for prayer and armor has led them to greater disciplines that help snap me back into reality. Most of all, I appreciate the way they stir up vision in me – and help me to see beyond the four walls I live inside – to a hurting and needy, lost world.

Here is the **Mission Team Principle:** We have the privilege of serving with others that are sometimes far away. We hurt with them, and pray for them, but they also add something – they help expand our vision beyond our own work.

Faithful Companions:

Paul made clear that *only **Luke** is with me...* (4:11a)

Years ago, Henry Durbanville wrote: "A friend is the first person who comes in when the whole world goes out." There is a delight in sending out people to ministry, but thankfully, some stay with us and cling to us. What a joy! Building a team in a small town has taught me that everyone who decides to remain and capture the local vision is a gift of God to us!

Not to wander, but let me say this: I keep hearing about Cyber-church, and part time shepherding, etc. We need to be careful and not to be so foolish as to think we can reinvent real companionship and relationship. The computer is a TOOL to reach into each other's lives, not a substitute. The electronic religion of the multitudes creates an emptiness — interpersonal relationships are so desperately needed to keep our faith glowing and growing, and not just in chat rooms... If you drop off your associations with other Christians and disassociate yourself from them in worship and service, you will run out of spiritual fervor and dedication in a short time.

Here is the **Companions Principle**: There is no relational substitute for sweating while laboring side by side with a friend.

The TRUTH of *Koinonia* is that God's family has some responsibility to and with one another...

- We are to be hospitable to one another – 1 Pet. 4:9 – being more than nice.
- We are to care for one another – 1 Cor. 12:26 – not lip service – but selfless service.
- We are to pray for one another – James 5:16 – not ignore one another.

- We are to restore one another – James 5:19-20 – not destroy each other.
- We are to teach and admonish one another – Col. 3:16 – teach where we can, correct where we must.
- We are to serve one another in love – Galatians 5:13 – giving of ourselves to one another.

The greatest hindrance I have observed in church ministry is NOT the behavior of lost men and women around us – but perpetually immature people among us. **Churches are CRIPPLED by spending hours settling disputes caused by immature people.**

Some need affirmation. They play games. They are willing to minister if they get the opportunity to be important and affirmed. They will be gone for a few weeks and then be upset that no one seemed to notice.

<u>Here is a truth: Get involved in ministry and people will know when you aren't there.</u> If you are not a vital part of keeping it moving, people may not notice if you absent yourself. Don't play games with busy people who are doing the work. It is immature, and it bogs down children's workers and deacons that are already taxed heavily with the size of the issues in front of them.

Ask yourself this:

- **Am I giving more than I expect to take in relationships with others in my church?**

If you are giving more, then ask this:

- **Am I hungering for attention and praise, or am I growing in maturity and serving the Lord for His praise?**

Perhaps in order to move my mind off my own troubles, I should learn to take notice of the cares and the joys of the fellow Christians around me. Maybe I am talking too much but listening too little. Maybe too many of my sentences are filled with "I" and "me." Listen to others; listen in order to help them. Often you won't even need to say anything. You don't have to fix all their problems – but you do have to care.

Let me deliberately encourage you to find an active role in the life of the family. Have you ever heard anyone say, "I can worship and be fed spiritually at home..."? They say that because they think church is for THEM. We are for each other, and all of us collectively are for HIM.

Don't forget to pray for those with special needs, mentioning them by name in your private prayers. Don't make prayer requests a matter of gossip, but keep prayer requests simple where they can be and confidential where they must be.

Restored Ones:

In the words at the end of *2 Timothy 4: 11: Pick up* **Mark** *and bring him with you, for he is useful to me for service...*

Paul made it clear that he recognized old conflicts needed to be laid to rest (4:11b).

Mark had a spotted past. Most scholars think he was the disciple that ran from the Garden of Gethsemane without his cloak. We know that he was a rich kid from a Cypriot Jewish home. We also know he left Paul on the earliest mission journey and his second attempt to come on board ended up splitting the team of Paul and Mark's uncle Barnabas – a painful moment in Paul's ministry. Here Paul called on Mark and made the point that he was profitable.

Now we see at work the **Restoration Principle:** Mistakes ARE made in ministry, and we need to recognize them and still love one another. Restoration is a central theme in God's salvation story!

Chuck Swindoll made the observation: "The neighborhood bar is possibly the best counterfeit that there is to the fellowship Christ wants us to give his church. It's an imitation, dispensing liquor instead of grace, escape rather than reality – but it is a permissive, accepting and inclusive fellowship. It is unshockable. It is democratic. You can tell people secrets, and they usually don't tell others or even want to. The bar flourishes not because most people are alcoholics, but because God has put into the human heart the desire to know and be known, to love and be loved, and so many seek a counterfeit at the price of a few beers."

Reinforcers:

Paul's reference included the man who apparently went to carry this very letter, 2 Timothy, to its recipient – Pastor Timothy at Ephesus. Paul recognized that Tim needed additional support (and this letter) in Ephesus, so Paul sent **Tychicus** (4:12).

The writer of proverbs says: *Proverbs 27:17 As iron sharpens iron, so one man sharpens another.*

Reinforcing friends help sharpen us to become spiritually acute a bit at a time. Think of a blacksmith who makes swords. He takes a hammer that is made out of iron and methodically beats another piece of iron, continuously landing blow by blow, until it takes the shape and sharpness of a sword. That isn't always comfortable for either side – the hammer or the sword – but the effect is worth the struggle.

We are better when we have reinforcing friends that can help shape us.

The sending of **Tychicus** illustrates the **Reinforcer Principle:** We all need those who will under gird and reinforce the work that God has laid on our hearts. Often our vision can only be accomplished when many hands and feet move! We have to SEE each other.

C.S. Lewis said something simple, but illuminating: "Friendship is born at that moment when one person says to another, 'What! You, too? I thought I was the only one.'"

Old Friends:

By this, I don't just mean friends that have been on the planet a long time, I mean friends that have known US a long time. Paul mentioned Priscilla and Aquila, the tent makers with the old battle scars from war fought alongside Paul (4:19) as did the worker **Onesiphorus** (literally, "profit bringer" – 4:19b) a member of the church who boldly supported and encouraged Paul in the past (1:16).

The little children's song says: Make new friends, but keep the OLD, one is silver and the other gold.

Psychology Today: "In a survey, more than 40,000 Americans said these qualities were most valued in a friend:

- The ability to keep confidences
- Loyalty
- Warmth and affection" (Quoted in *Homemade*, June 1982.)

Proverbs 17:17: A friend loves at all times and a brother is born for adversity.

Friends are committed for seasons; great friends are committed for life.

The **Old Friend Principle** is this: Build a life team – a corps of people that you stay in contact with over the years to mutually pray for and encourage each other. Even at the end of his life, Paul wanted them to know that he had not forgotten them. Friends stick and though the days with them slip away, they live in our hearts.

Supporters:

2 Timothy 4:20 Erastus remained at Corinth, but Trophimus I left sick at Miletus."

Erastus, the city treasurer of Corinth (Rom. 16:23) was not able to be present, but aided the ministry in his own abilities. He couldn't GO, but he could GIVE (4:20). Some people like **Trophimus** are God-provided supporters unable to follow due to the failing of their body (4:20) but they desired to be faithful.

The **Supporter Principle** is this: Sometimes the most meaningful and needed friends aren't the ones on the battle line, but the ones on the supply line.

Look at the local church that was Paul's support base: surrounded by believers who made a difference, Paul wrote:

*2 Timothy 4:21 ...**Eubulus** greets you, also **Pudens** and **Linus** and **Claudia** and all the brethren.*

Writing to another church the YOU is plural in the end of the letter – showing Paul's intent was public reading for this personal letter. Acts 2:42 says the early Christians devoted themselves to fellowship. They just didn't HAVE fellowship; **they devoted themselves to it. This means that fellowship was a priority and one of the objectives for gathering together.**

Focus on The Word:

To keep a people focus, we will need frequent correction and instruction – even if we have walked with God for many years. I LOVE that Paul's final comments went PAST PEOPLE. He loved the team, and he knew ministry was about people – but that is NOT the only eternal value we are to have! Look at what he asked Tim to bring him.

2 Timothy 4:13 When you come bring the cloak which I left at Troas with Carpus, and the books, especially the parchments.

Though Paul requested his letter writing equipment, he particularly wanted the parchments – The Word of God (4:13). He didn't know how long he had to live, but he knew what message warmed his faith and kept him digging into LIFE…God's Word.

Focus on Intimacy with God:

We have seen Paul focused on PEOPLE and he expressed his hunger for the Word – but the final words of the Apostle also included two very important little sentences that lay open his heart:

2 Timothy 4:17 But the Lord stood with me and strengthened me, so that through me the proclamation might be fully accomplished, and that all the Gentiles might hear; and I was rescued out of the lion's mouth. 18 The Lord will rescue me from every evil deed, and will bring me safely to His heavenly kingdom; to Him be the glory forever and ever. Amen.

Paul was able to say it clearly:

- God stands with me when I am alone (4:17a).

- God gives me the strength to complete the work He has commissioned (4:17b).
- God rescues me from the snare of the enemy (lion – 4:17b).
- God delivers me safely to His home (4:18).
- God is worthy of praise for all the ages! (4:18b)

As we face the end of life's journey, our real values come out. I recall the old story:

"Eleven millionaires went down on the Titanic. One wealthy man, Major A. H. Peuchen left $300,000.00 in money, jewelry and securities in a box in his cabin. 'The money seemed a mockery at that time,' he later said. 'I picked up three oranges instead.'" (Source Unknown)

Paul shared his end values:

God's best work is accomplished in followers who learn to focus on the three eternal parts of life: people, the Word and intimacy with God.

Other volumes in the series through the Bible are available through amazon.com and can be found by searching for:

"Dr. Randall D. Smith"

Free teaching resources are also available at:

www.randalldsmith.com

www.ingramcontent.com/pod-product-compliance
Lightning Source LLC
Chambersburg PA
CBHW060518030426

42337CB00015B/1934